Coffeetime in Winter

Bible-based Reflections for Each Day of the Season

MY COFFEE-CUP MEDITATIONS

Coffeetime in Winter

Bible-based Reflections for Each Day of the Season

ROGER ELLSWORTH

This edition 2022 Coffeetime in Winter
ISBN 978-1-63342-281-0

Shepherd Press
P.O. Box 24
Wapwallopen, PA 18660

www.shepherdpress.com

www.mycoffeecup meditations.com

www.rogerellsworth.org

Purpose

My Coffee Cup Meditations are short, easy-to-read, engagingly presented devotions based on the Bible, the Word of God. Each reading takes a single idea or theme and develops it in a thought-provoking way so that you are inspired to consider the greatness of God, the relevance of the good news of the life, death, resurrection, and coming-again of Jesus, and are better equipped for life in this world and well prepared for the world to come.

www.mycoffeecupmeditations.com

https://www.facebook.com/MyCoffeeCupMeditations/

We hope you will enjoy these Bible-based meditations. We would love to hear from you, so please send us a note to tell us what you think—which ones you liked most, and how they made a difference in your life or in the life of a family member, friend, or work associate.

To reach us online, go to
www.mycoffeecupmeditations.com/contact

We offer quantity discounts for bulk quantity purchases.
Contact us for more details.

Be sure to collect each of the four volumes in this series!

Coffeetime in Winter: 978-1-63342-281-0
Coffeetime in Spring: 978-1-63342-282-7
Coffeetime in Summer: 978-1-63342-283-4
Coffeetime in Autumn: 978-1-63342-284-1

About the Authors

Roger Ellsworth is a retired pastor, active in ministry and writing, who lives in Jackson, Tennessee. He and his wife, Sylvia, love the message of the Bible, and they enjoy sharing the wonderful counsel of the Word of God in language that ordinary people can understand and appreciate. Roger has written numerous books on the Christian faith, and has exercised a preaching ministry for over fifty years.

Roger and Sylvia have two sons, Tim and Martyn, who have also contributed devotions to this volume.

Introduction: All About this Series

From God's Word, the Bible...

Blessed is the man
Who walks not in the counsel of the ungodly,
Nor stands in the path of sinners,
Nor sits in the seat of the scornful;
But his delight is in the law of the Lord,
And in His law he meditates day and night.
He shall be like a tree
Planted by the rivers of water,
That brings forth its fruit in its season,
Whose leaf also shall not wither;
And whatever he does shall prosper.

Psalm 1:1-3

What you have here is the first part of what was produced as a big book—twelve books all in one, in fact. The idea of connecting enjoying coffee and reading the Bible devotionally happened early in 2017 when I wrote the first book in what became a series of *My Coffee-Cup Meditations*.

Early mornings are very predictable for lots and lots of Christians. Roll out of bed, turn on the coffee pot, pour a cup, settle into a favorite chair and enjoy what is called "the daily devotional." This usually consists of reading a passage from the Bible and a selection from a devotional book. It concludes with prayer.

Christians who follow this pattern can go through a good bit of devotional material as the years go by. So they are always looking for new material—something to go along with their Bible and their coffee.

Hoping that I could be helpful in supplying the need for more devotional material, I gathered up some articles I had written and put them in a book—*A Dog and a Clock*. The idea was to supply brothers and sisters in Christ with enough devotions to carry them through one month. That quickly led to another book—*The Thumbs Up Man*—to carry "devotion-doers" through another month and then another.

You can guess what happened after three or four books came out. There are twelve months in the year. So why not provide enough books to cover a year? So off we went and out the books came until there were finally twelve books, each with thirty-one readings! Since these books were designed to go with the Bible and a good cup of coffee, it seemed right to call them *My Coffee-Cup Meditations*. Thanks to my good friends Jim and Sue Holmes for that suggestion! And thanks to my wife, Sylvia, and my sons, Tim and Martyn, for contributing some chapters along the way.

Then came the idea of producing the books together, so that there would be enough readings for a whole year, and with some left over, as not all months have thirty-one days. So the result is that we combined all twelve of the books into one big one: *The Big Book of Coffee Cup Meditations*! That way, people would be able to read from whichever month they wished to at any time in the year—and never have too few days in the month, because there would always be thirty-one readings in each month!

We thought and prayed about how to present these books in yet another format, the idea of Bible readings for each of the seasons of the year came to mind: Coffeetime in Winter, Spring, Summer, and Fall. And so it is that you are holding the first of the set of four books in your hand!

One of my main concerns in writing these books was to cause the gospel of our Lord Jesus Christ to shine. It's wrong to think that the gospel is for unbelievers only. Believers need the gospel! We need to be reminded again and again of the greatness of what our Lord Jesus Christ did for us in His life, death, resurrection, and ascension. The more we ponder the gospel and the more deeply we ponder it, the more we will find our hearts flooded with gratitude, and the more willing we will be to faithfully serve Him.

My Coffee-Cup Meditations are published for you with the hope that you will read the devotions, enjoy them, and, most of all, find that you are inspired to consider the greatness of God, the relevance of the good news of the life, death, resurrection, and coming-again of Jesus, and are better equipped for life in this world and well prepared for the world to come.

And don't forget to pour that cup of coffee!

A Dog and A Clock

... And 30 Other Bible-Based Meditations

The dog of Angelo del Plato watched intently as his master was lowered into the grave. Eight years later, friends of the family acknowledged that they could not remember a day when that loving dog did not visit his master's gravesite, usually sitting a while on the turf over his master's body. . . Even those who are not dog lovers must admire and commend the faithfulness of that dog to his master. It is a sharp rebuke to many Christians for their lack of faithfulness to their Master!

Contents

A Dog and A Clock

From God's Word, the Bible...

Do not fear any of those things which you are about to suffer. Indeed, the devil is about to throw some of you into prison, that you may be tested, and you will have tribulation ten days. Be faithful until death, and I will give you the crown of life.

Revelation 2:10

Being a lover of dogs, I was moved by these lines I came across from an old issue of a Christian news magazine that I was reading:

The dog of Angelo del Plato watched intently as his master was lowered into the grave. Eight years later, friends of the family acknowledged that they could not remember a day when that loving dog did not visit his master's gravesite, usually sitting a while on the turf over his master's body.

Even those who are not dog lovers must admire and commend the faithfulness of that dog to his master. It is a sharp rebuke to many Christians for their lack of faithfulness to their Master!

Yes, all Christians have a Master—the Lord Jesus Christ! Tell me that you do not regard Jesus as your Master, and I will not hesitate to tell you that you are not a Christian! I do so on no less authority than that of the Apostle Paul: "If anyone does not love the Lord Jesus Christ, let him be accursed. . ." (1 Cor. 16:22).

I'm sure that Angelo del Plato did much to win the affection of his dog. He undoubtedly fed him, talked to him, played with him, walked with him, and cared for him when he was sick.

The question I have for my fellow-believers is simply this: Has your Master, the Lord Jesus Christ, done less for you than del Plato did for his dog? Every Christian must immediately utter a resounding "No!" to that question. The Lord Jesus has done infinitely more for us than del Plato did for his dog! The Lord Jesus has rescued us from the wrath of God by receiving that wrath in our stead. He has forgiven us of our sins. He has made us part of the family of God. He has given us countless blessings and benefits to make life more comfortable and pleasant. And He has promised to eventually take us home to Himself to share in His eternal glory. What more could the Lord Jesus do for us?

We should frequently remind ourselves of these words from Jesus: "But why do you call me 'Lord, Lord,' and do not do the things which I say?" (Luke 6:46).

The issue facing each of us is whether we will be as faithful to our Master as del Plato's dog was to him. Or will we commend in a dog that which we refuse to practice ourselves?

My wife and I have moved a lot in our years together. One item always receives special attention when we move. It is our Seth Thomas clock. I awoke a few minutes before four o'clock the other day and heard the steady ticking of that old clock. I listened as it sounded four times. I thought for a while about what I was hearing. That clock is well over a hundred years of age, and it is still faithfully ticking and sounding.

I cannot say how many moves I have left before my final move. But I know I must emulate that clock. I must faithfully tick until my last moving day comes.

I know I cannot do this apart from the gracious help of the Lord. So these days I find myself saying:

Change and decay all around I see,
O Thou who changest not, abide with me.
(Henry F. Lyte)

Whenever I am Afraid

From God's Word, the Bible...

The Lord is my light and my salvation;
Whom shall I fear?
The Lord is the strength of my life;
Of whom shall I be afraid?

I sought the Lord, and He heard me,
And delivered me from all my fears.

In the multitude of my anxieties within me,
Your comforts delight my soul.

Psalm 27:1; Psalm 34:4; Psalm 94:19

In Psalm 56:3, David admits to being afraid. To be afraid is to be "filled with fear or apprehension." That word "afraid" is all too familiar! We are often filled with fear and apprehension.

Most of our fears have to do with our lives or the lives of those we love either being lessened in quality or coming to an end.

Many things can lessen the quality of our lives or the lives of our loved ones—sickness, financial reversals, family discord, world conditions, and many other things. There is no shortage of things to bring about apprehension!

And the biggest one of all is death itself! How many people have proudly marched through life as if they were in control and as if they were sufficient for everything, only to tremble and cower when they came to death's door! Haughty and proud in his disdain for Christianity, skeptic David Hume whimpered at death: "I am affrighted and confounded with the forlorn solitude in which I am placed by my philosophy. . . I fancy myself in the most deplorable condition imaginable, environed in the deepest darkness."

The David who wrote Psalm 56:3 was the man who stood fearlessly before Goliath. But he was "very much afraid" when he took up his pen to write this psalm. He was in the land of the Philistines, where he did not belong, and it seemed to him that King Achish would soon snuff out his life (see 1 Sam. 21:12). But David collected himself, looked to God, and wrote: "Whenever I am afraid, I will trust in You."

"Whenever" means "at whatever time," or "at any or every time." In Psalm 56:3, it is a beautiful word! At whatever time or at any time David finds himself gripped with fear, he will trust in God. Every time he is afraid, he will trust God. Trusting is always the great antidote for fearing.

Are you, like David and so many others, frightened by the thought of death? Trust in God! He has both made glorious promises regarding death and has shown Himself to be utterly faithful to His promises.

What has God promised about this matter of death? He has promised His people will not face it alone, that He Himself will meet them in the "valley of the shadow" and will shepherd them safely through (Ps. 23:4). He has promised that at the very moment of death, the souls of His people will go immediately into His presence (2 Cor. 5:6-8). And He has promised that the bodies of all those who belong to Him will finally be raised from their graves, rejoined to their souls, and will forever be with Him in eternal glory (1 Thess. 4:13-18).

What promises! But please note that these are promises God has given only to His people! Not all are His people. Those who are not in a right relationship with Him have His promise that they will face Him in judgment and will be driven forever from His presence (2 Thess. 1:8-10). That will cause any thinking person to really be afraid! (Luke 12:4-5).

Are you afraid of that immensely sobering time when you will have to stand before God in judgment? God has given a promise for you to trust. He has promised that He will forgive all those who trust completely in His Son, Jesus Christ, and in what He did on the cross for sinners like you and me (John 3:16,36; 5:24; 6:47; 1 John 5:11-12).

Those who believe in Jesus can rejoice in these words from the Apostle Paul: "There is therefore now no condemnation to those who are in Christ Jesus..." (Rom. 8:1).

Afraid? Don't be! Trust God's promise to save sinners and then trust His promises to take care of His people. Make it your policy to say to God: "Whenever I am afraid, I will trust in You."

"He, to Rescue Me from Danger, Interposed His Precious Blood"

From God's Word, the Bible...

And if you call on the Father, who without partiality judges according to each one's work, conduct yourselves throughout the time of your stay here in fear; knowing that you were not redeemed with corruptible things, like silver or gold, from your aimless conduct received by tradition from your fathers, but with the precious blood of Christ, as of a lamb without blemish and without spot. He indeed was foreordained before the foundation of the world, but was manifest in these last times for you.

1 Peter 1:17-20

Jesus sought me when a stranger,
Wandering from the fold of God;
He, to rescue me from danger,
Interposed His precious blood...
(Come, Thou Fount of Every Blessing, Robert Robinson, 1758)

These words take us to the heart of Christ's saving work on behalf of His people. It was a matter of Jesus interposing His blood! That act of interposition makes His blood precious to every believer.

More about that in a moment! First, let's think about that word "danger." Frightening word! When we hear the word "danger," we tend to think of the people and the things that threaten our wellbeing and happiness in this world. There is no shortage of them.

There is, however, another type of danger which is much worse than any posed by this temporal realm. It is the danger of experiencing the wrath of God in eternity. People these days like to play down that danger, but no fair reading of the Bible will allow us to do so. All are agreed that the Old Testament places a heavy emphasis on the matter, but we must not think that the teaching of God's wrath is confined there. The same teaching is evenly distributed throughout the New Testament. It is in the Gospels (Matt. 3:12; 7:13-14; 22:13-14; 23:33; 25:30,41,46; Mark 9:42-29; Luke 16:19-31; John 3:36), in the epistles of Paul (Rom. 1:18-19; 2:5; 3:5; 4:15; 12:19; Eph. 2:3; 5:6), and in the other epistles as well (Heb. 10:27; 12:25-29; James 5:9; 1 Peter 4:17-18; 2 Peter 2:4-9).

It is the dominant theme of the book of Revelation (Rev. 6:16-17; 11:18; 14:10,19; 15:1,7; 16:1,19; 19:15; 20:11-15; 21:8; 22:11,15).

And for those who blissfully say: "Just give me the loving God of John 3:16," the wrath of God is powerfully present in the word "perish" which is mentioned in that very verse.

We will never understand Christianity until we realize that it is all about rescuing people from this danger! Jesus came to this world for the express purpose of dealing with that danger.

God is holy. He cannot merely ignore our sins as if they never happened. He has to pronounce a sentence on them and also has to carry out that sentence. What is His sentence on our sins? It is His wrath, which is eternal separation from Himself in hell.

The glory of Christianity is that Jesus on the cross took the wrath that we deserve for our sins. There He "interposed" or inserted His blood between the wrath of God and guilty sinners. The word "blood" means that He poured out His life in death. To say He interposed His blood is to say He interposed Himself. On the cross He took the position between the wrath of God and guilty sinners. The wrath fell on Him, and there is now no wrath left for all who repent of their sins and trust in Him. John 3:36 puts it perfectly: "He who believes in the Son has everlasting life; and he who does not believe the Son shall not see life, but the wrath of God abides on him."

But how could Jesus in the space of the six hours that He was on the cross (from 9:00 in the morning until 3:00 in the afternoon) receive an eternity's worth of the wrath of God for all sinners who believe in Him? The answer lies in the special nature of Jesus. He was no ordinary man. He was the God-man, fully God, fully man at one and the same time. As God, He was an infinite person, and as an infinite person, He could receive in a finite length of time an infinite measure of wrath. In other words, Jesus as an infinite person could receive in a finite measure of time what we as finite people would receive in an infinite measure of time.

When we truly understand what Jesus did on the cross for sinners, we gladly respond to Robert Robinson's phrase "precious blood" with a hearty "Yes!"

January 4

Tell Me What You Think You Owe...

FROM GOD'S WORD, THE BIBLE...

"Therefore I say to you, her sins, which are many, are forgiven, for she loved much. But to whom little is forgiven, the same loves little."
Then He said to her, "Your sins are forgiven."
And those who sat at the table with Him began to say to themselves, "Who is this who even forgives sins?"
Then He said to the woman, "Your faith has saved you. Go in peace."

FROM LUKE 7:36-50

Tell me what you think you owe the Lord, and I will tell you how much you feel like serving Him. If you think you owe a great deal, you will gladly serve and worship Him. If you think you owe very little, you will not be much interested in service or worship.

The truth of the matter is every Christian owes the Lord the same amount. He has done no less for one than He has for others. We all come into this world in a very sad and sorrowful condition. We come in with a sinful nature that causes us to be alienated or separated from God.

The piercing question is this: How can sinful human beings ever hope to enjoy fellowship with the perfectly holy God? To put it another way, how can guilty sinners ever stand acceptably in the presence of the holy God?

The answer is that sin must be taken out of the way, and there is only one way that sin can be removed from between God and us. Its penalty has to be paid! What is the penalty for sin? It is eternal separation from God or the eternal wrath of God!

There are only two ways for the penalty for our sins to be paid: we either have to pay it ourselves, which means we must be separated from God and heaven forever, or someone has to pay it on our behalf. In order for someone else to pay the penalty for our sins, such a person must, of course, be free from sin. We see the logic of this. If someone has sins of his own, he would have to pay the penalty for those and could not, therefore, pay the penalty for anyone else.

Jesus is the only person who ever lived without sin (John 1:14; 1 Peter 1:19; 1 John 3:5). Because He had no sins of His own, He could pay for the sins of others.

This is what His death on the cross is all about. There He received the wrath of God in the place of sinners. Because He was God in human flesh, He could receive in a finite length of time an infinite measure of wrath. This is the reason He cried out from the cross: "My God, My God, why have You forsaken Me?" (Matt. 27:46).

The cost of sin is God-forsakenness in hell, and, on that cross, Jesus endured God-forsakenness for sinners. All who realize the depth and guilt of their sins and entrust themselves fully to Jesus in the work He did on the cross are released from the sentence of God's wrath (John 3:16,36; Rom. 5:8-9;1 Thess. 1:10; 1 Peter 2:24).

What do Christians owe the Lord? A debt that can never be paid! We have been delivered from the wrath of God and given eternal life through Christ. In referring to a debt we owe, I am not suggesting that we must work for our salvation. Not for a moment! The Apostle Paul says: "For by grace you have been saved through faith, and that not of yourselves; it is the gift of God, not of works, lest anyone should boast" (Eph. 2:8-9).

We do not work *for* our salvation but *from* our salvation. Because we have been saved by the redeeming death of the Lord Jesus, we work to show our love and gratitude to Him.

It is not easy to show gratitude to the Lord by worshiping and serving Him. There are always a thousand things to occupy us. Some people excuse themselves from worship and service because they feel that they don't have the time. Other people do so because they have been offended or hurt. Yet others do so because they don't agree with the direction the church is going.

The answer to each of these excuses is the same: What do you owe? If you say that you owe nothing less than deliverance from the wrath of God to Christ, you must surely go on to say that He is worthy of your time and energy and that no hurt or disagreement is great enough to offset the debt.

What I have been saying is pointedly expressed in these words from Isaac Watts:

When I survey the wondrous cross
On which the Prince of Glory died,
My richest gain I count but loss,
And pour contempt on all my pride.

Forbid it, Lord, that I should boast,
Save in the death of Christ my God;
All the vain things that charm me most –
I sacrifice them to His blood.

Were the whole realm of nature mine,
That were a present far too small:
Love so amazing, so divine,
Demands my soul, my life, my all.

The Passing of a Celebrity

From God's Word, the Bible...

And as it is appointed for men to die once, but after this the judgment, so Christ was offered once to bear the sins of many. To those who eagerly wait for Him He will appear a second time, apart from sin, for salvation.

Hebrews 9:27-28

Michael Jackson is dead. At one time, he had great wealth. He still had great fame when he breathed his last. But now he is gone.

In reporting his death, one newsperson continued to express shock that this famous man had died at age fifty. It was as if he, the newsman, was assuming that one has to be a certain age to die!

But death is all around us all the time. We are reminded of it when we drive by a cemetery, hospital or nursing facility, or when we see an obituary column.

Death takes young and old, rich and poor, the well educated and the illiterate, conservative and liberal. The greatest fact of life is death. Martin Luther was right in saying the following words: "Life is a constant and daily journey toward death. One after another dies, and the living must merely engage in the miserable business of carrying one another to the grave. All of us are traveling the same road together."

The Bible tells us that the wise man thinks about what lies ahead and makes prudent preparation for it (Prov. 22:3). The fool never does.

If death is inevitable, is it not wise to think about it and prepare for it?

But how many there are who seem to think life is sure and death is uncertain. Just the opposite is true!

Many people, these days, would argue that there is nothing for which to prepare because death is the end. Really? Isn't there something inside you that screams that it is not so?

The Bible tells us that we were made by God and for God and we must meet God. It flatly says: "Prepare to meet your God. . .!" (Amos 4:12).

But how do we prepare for death? The Bible has the answer for that as well. It tells us to repent of our sins and to take the Lord Jesus Christ as our Savior. Why take Jesus? He has demonstrated His authority over death by rising from the grave.

If you don't know how to handle something, the best thing to do is go to someone who does know how to handle it. You and I are not able to handle death and what lies beyond it, but the Lord Jesus is able. If we place ourselves in His hands, we have nothing to fear about death or the hereafter.

But we must truly take Jesus as our Savior and not just go through the motions of doing so. If we really trust Him, it will show up in our lives. We will not try to govern our lives with no regard for Him, for His Book (the Bible), for His day (the Lord's Day), or for His church. Many who think they have received Christ have only deceived themselves.

I have come to love a song that urges people to come to Jesus and "laugh on glory's side." There is indeed a glory side for those who receive Christ. It is called heaven. And Jesus is the way! If you want to take the fear out of death and "laugh on glory's side," turn to Christ now.

Because we never know when death will come, sooner is always better than later for fleeing to Christ.

January 6

Two Questions Most Church Attendees Dare Not Ask Themselves

FROM GOD'S WORD, THE BIBLE...

Do not fear any of those things which you are about to suffer. Indeed, the devil is about to throw some of you into prison, that you may be tested, and you will have tribulation ten days. Be faithful until death, and I will give you the crown of life.

REVELATION 2:10

Practically every church in my city of Jackson, Tennessee, cancelled services on May 2, 2010, because of the flood that brought about fifteen inches of rain to our area. My church was among those that canceled. So I sat at home that day and watched a lot of religious TV programming. As I viewed program after program, I was astonished at how little of the gospel I heard. Most of the messages focused on how to make life in this world more enjoyable and comfortable. It was much like watching Oprah or Dr. Phil!

I admit that the Bible does say a good bit about living in this world, but it is always does so in connection with the gospel and as a consequence of the gospel. It was a clear statement of the gospel that was so noticeably missing in most of the programs I viewed. So I found myself thinking about two questions that most church attendees dare not ask themselves. The first is this: Is what I am getting from my church real Christianity? Christianity is not just a successful living technique. It is the declaration of what God has done in and through Jesus to rescue sinners from their sins and the wrath to come and to give them right standing with God and eternal glory.

There is no Christianity without the gospel, and if you are in a church that doesn't emphasize the gospel, you are not really in a church at all.

That led me to a second question: If I am not getting real Christianity from my church, why am I supporting it?

Some would say it is because there is so much "energy" in the services. However, the prophets of Baal had lots and lots of energy, and they were horribly wrong (1 Kings 18:25-28).

Some would say it is because the church offers so many activities for the children. The Bible says parents are to bring their children up in the teaching of the Lord! No parent can discharge this responsibility if he has his children in a church that does not preach the gospel.

Some would say it is because the crowd is so large. But the Bible tells us not to follow a crowd to do evil (Exod. 23:2).

On the rainy day as I sat at home, I also found myself thinking about another day—the day of God's judgment. How sad it will be for many so-called Christian pastors to stand in the presence of the Lord and be faced with the enormous realization that they had never really preached Christianity at all! (1 Cor. 3:10-17). And how very sad it will be on that day for the multitudes of professing Christians to realize that they had spent most of their lives going to churches where they never really heard the Christian message at all!

If you had asked me on that day if we needed the flood, I would have said: "No way!"

But if you were to ask me today if I can think of a flood that we do need, I would answer with an emphatic yes. We need a spiritual flood, the flood depicted in these words:

Rain down, you heavens, from above,
And let the skies pour down righteousness;
Let the earth open, let them bring forth salvation,
And let righteousness spring up together.
(Isa. 45:8)

Such a flood would sweep away that which is false and flimsy, and restore the gospel to the priority it deserves.

Christianity or "Ianity"?

From God's Word, the Bible...

God forbid that I should boast except in the cross of our Lord Jesus Christ, by whom the world has been crucified to me, and I to the world.

Galatians 6:14

The Apostle Paul was not in doubt about what he should preach. He put it very clearly: "I determined not to know anything among you except Jesus Christ and Him crucified" (1 Cor. 2:2).

It's obvious that Paul was a preacher of Christianity. The word "Christianity" has Christ in it, and Paul preached Christ.

Many preachers these days cannot echo the words of Paul. They are not preachers of Christ, and if we take Christ out of Christianity, we have something called "Ianity."

Isn't it interesting that "Ianity" begins with "I"? Much of what we call Christianity these days has very little to do with Christ and a lot to do with us. Our worship is not about Christ and His great deeds. It is about us and how we feel about things. And our great concern is not serving God. It is rather getting God to serve us. We don't want to fall before Him as our Sovereign. We want Him to be our helper with all the little aggravations and challenges that life brings our way. These are the days of the "troubleshooter" God. We don't want much to do with Him, but we want Him to be ready to spring into action if we need Him!

Maybe He can keep our children from spilling their milk or keep the dog from coming into the house with muddy feet!

We don't want a God who talks about sin. That would make us feel bad! And we aren't all that interested in heaven. We want our best life now!

The thing we so often fail to see is that the smaller we make God, the more unnecessary we make Him! Many these days are starved for the greatness of God. If they were to speak to our churches, they might very well say: "We will take care of the milk and the dog; give us a God that can do for us what we cannot do for ourselves."

What is it we cannot do for ourselves? We can't rid ourselves of sin, lift from ourselves the sentence of God's condemnation, or prepare ourselves to stand acceptably in the presence of a holy God. But through the Lord Jesus Christ, God forgives sinners, cancels the sentence of condemnation, and declares those sinners to be guiltless. While so many pursue the God who specializes in trivia, the Bible calls us to pursue the God who specializes in salvation. This is Christianity!

Some time ago, Michael Horton, a professor in California, wrote a book entitled *Christless Christianity*. Some undoubtedly responded to that title by saying: "That's nonsense. You can't have Christianity with Christ!" And that is the sharp point of the book! When you take Christ out of Christianity, you have something, but it is no longer Christianity. Let's just call it "Ianity," which, by the way, is only one letter, the letter "n," away from "inanity," that is "a lack of substance" or "shallowness."

There you have it! Christianity without Christ is shallow and empty.

While it professes to be profound, it is far from it.

There are two things that every true believer in Christ should dread above everything else. One is a Christless Bible and the other is a crossless Christ. "Ianity" offers us both! It takes Christ out of the Bible and makes it some sort of miscellaneous collection of tips and guidelines for living better, and when "Ianity" does give us one of its infrequent mentions of Christ, it is not the Christ who endured the wrath of God on the cross for sinners. It is, rather, the Christ who helps us implement the tips! Christianity, on the other hand, rightly sees Christ as the subject of the whole Bible (Luke 24:27,44) and rightly emphasizes that Christ came to this earth to die on that cross, and that there is no hope for salvation except in that redeeming death.

January 8

The Danger of Snapshot Theology

From God's Word, the Bible…

Do not fret because of evildoers,
Nor be envious of the workers of iniquity.
For they shall soon be cut down like the grass,
And wither as the green herb.
Trust in the Lord, and do good;
Dwell in the land, and feed on His faithfulness.
Delight yourself also in the Lord,
And He shall give you the desires of your heart.

From Psalm 37:1-11

The Christian life is not easy! Anyone who tells you that it is, doesn't know what he's talking about. The Lord Jesus tells us that following Him means denying ourselves and carrying a cross (Matt. 16:24). The Apostle Paul tells us that the Christian life is a warfare (Eph. 6:10-20).

Sometimes, however, we make the Christian life harder than it needs to be. Living for the Lord is much easier when we trust the Lord to always have our best interests at heart and to always be with us in every difficult circumstance. It becomes immensely more difficult when we doubt these things.

Sadly enough, many Christians do doubt that God really cares for them. They are disappointed with Him. He has not lived up to their expectations.

One thing that inevitably leads to disappointment with God is what I call "snapshot theology." What is snapshot theology? It is drawing conclusions about God on the basis of the circumstances in which we find ourselves at this moment.

How easy it is to do this! We often find that our circumstances are a lot less desirable than we would have them to be, and on the basis of those circumstances we conclude that God has failed us. We can be sure that the devil is ever eager to help us draw that conclusion. He is very quick to speak along these lines: "If God truly loved you, you wouldn't have these problems."

I have often said that if we begin with the wrong job description for God, He will always fail in our eyes. If we assume that it is God's job to make life as comfortable for us as it can possibly be, we are bound to think ill of Him when our lives are not comfortable. But the problem is not with God; it is rather with our wrong thinking about Him. God has never told us that His purpose is to make life easy for us.

What is His purpose? It is to conform us to the image of His Son

(Rom. 8:29). In other words, it is to bring us to spiritual maturity.

Thank God, the trials of this life will someday come to an end. The tide of time will wash up on the shore of eternity. There, in the glory of God's presence, we will have a new and different perspective on the problems of this life. There we will not simply look at one snapshot from our lives, but God will rather show us the whole movie. As we are made aware of all that God was accomplishing in our lives, we will certainly find that our disappointment with Him has vanished and we will be lost in "wonder, love and praise."

It may be hard for us to believe now, but the truth of the matter is this: when God's people get home to glory and there see how He worked in their lives, their testimony will be: "He has done all things well."

The business before us is to simply trust even when we do not understand. We must trust God's *heart* even when we cannot trace His *hand*. No Christian should ever be in doubt about the heart of God. He put it clearly on display when He nailed His Son to the cross to die for our sins. As hard as it is to believe, the fact is our difficult circumstances do not mean God's heart has changed. Those difficulties come from that same heart of love.

Cookie the Christmas Dog and the Repackaging of Christmas

From God's Word, the Bible...

Then the angel said to them, "Do not be afraid, for behold, I bring you good tidings of great joy which will be to all people. For there is born to you this day in the city of David a Savior, who is Christ the Lord. And this will be the sign to you: You will find a Babe wrapped in swaddling cloths, lying in a manger."
And suddenly there was with the angel a multitude of the heavenly host praising God and saying:
"Glory to God in the highest,
And on earth peace, goodwill toward men!"

From Luke 2:8-14

Years ago, Sylvia and I had a dog named Cookie. She was a delight. I still miss her. Cookie was our Christmas dog and she loved Christmas.

One year Sylvia and I returned home to find that Cookie had opened some of the Christmas presents! Suffice it to say, it was necessary for us to do some repackaging.

But there is some Christmas re-packaging these days that is not necessary. Let me explain.

Most church leaders want to see their churches grow in membership and in attendance. I say "most" because I have met a few folks down through the years who preferred for the church to stay small. In one of my previous pastorates, a deacon got upset because our church was growing so much! Imagine that! I think he had a Diotrephes problem (see 3 John 9).

The other extreme consists of those who are willing to do anything to see their churches grow. This is the explanation for much of modern-day Christendom, which is in the grip of what may be called a sinister sequence.

This sequence begins with church leaders asking this question: "What can we do to get our church to grow?"

The answer to that question often amounts to this: We must get people to like us! The reasoning here is that if people like us, they will want to be around us, and if they want to be around us, they will come to church.

That, of course, leads to yet another question: What can we do to get people to like us?

And the answer to that is often along these lines: We must give them what they want and stop giving them things they don't want.

It doesn't take a lot of research to determine that people these days don't want to hear about sin, judgment to come or a man dying on a cross. So we must get rid of these things! Out with them! We must not allow ourselves to be troubled by the fact that for centuries these very things were considered to be the essential, non-negotiable core of Christianity! We must repackage Christianity into something that is marketable today!

When the repackaging is done, we have a Christianity that is more like a successful-living philosophy. We tell people to believe in Jesus so they can be happy in this life. The one fact that the re-packagers seem to be unwilling to face is this: there are plenty of non-Christians who are very happy with their lives! So when we tell them to accept Jesus to be happy, they simply smile and say, "No, thank you. We're already quite happy without Jesus. You may need Him, but we don't. So keep Him to yourself."

The truth of the matter is that many people today are presenting the Christian message in such a way that they are giving others a perfectly good reason for rejecting it.

But do we not run into the same problem when we tell people that they need Jesus because they are sinners? Can they not merely say that they don't feel like they are sinners and, therefore, do not need Jesus? Yes, they can say it, but the evidence is against them, and the voice of conscience tells them that the evidence is against them!

The church today finds herself in the peculiar position of telling people they need Jesus as their Savior after she, the church, has removed from her teaching any reason for people to need a Savior.

When we next approach the Christmas season, we would do well to reflect deeply on the words the angel spoke to Joseph: ". . .you shall call His name JESUS, for He will save His people from their sins" (Matt. 1:21).

Only sinners need saving. Since we are all sinners (Rom. 3:23), we all need saving. The good news of Christmas is that the Savior has come into the world. His name is Jesus. And He will save all those who see the reality and enormity of their sins and come to Him for saving.

January 10

And the Award for "Best-Dressed" Goes to...

From God's Word, the Bible...

For He made Him who knew no sin to be sin for us, that we might become the righteousness of God in Him.

2 Corinthians 5:21

Part of the silliness that surrounds the Oscar Awards each year is the prolonged discussion about the way in which the actors and actresses are dressed.

I recently came across this discussion on the TV Guide Channel. I was checking the listings, and there it was—two men and two women discussing, for the most part, the way in which the actresses were dressed. I didn't stay watching it for long, but it did get me to thinking again about the shallowness of this age.

It also got me to thinking again about how people are so absorbed with things that are passing that they give absolutely no thought to those things that last.

Take this matter of dress, for instance. The Bible teaches us that we must all leave this world and stand before God. It tells us that before we can enter into heaven we must be dressed in perfect righteousness.

It further tells us that we do not possess this righteousness ourselves. Because of our sinfulness, we are clothed in filthy rags.

But the good news of the Bible is this: we do not have to stand before the holy God in our filthy rags. By His righteous living, the Lord Jesus provided the garment that God demands. That garment of perfect righteousness can and will be ours if, while we are still in this life, we come to God and ask Him to grant us the perfect righteousness of Christ.

Eternal dress is far more important than temporal dress, but how very, very many people there are who concern themselves exclusively with the latter. They remind me of the Roman soldiers at the crucifixion of Jesus who gambled for His garments. Shockingly, they were gambling for temporal garments while being completely oblivious to the garment of salvation that Jesus was providing on that cross.

Those who go all through life thinking only about temporal things are in for a rude awakening. This is pictured for us in Matthew 22:1-14 which tells us that there will come a day when those who are not clothed in the perfect righteousness of Christ will be discovered and cast out of God's kingdom forever. May God help you to see the importance of receiving the righteousness of Christ.

As I listened to the boring discussion about the best-dressed actresses, I could not help but say: "The award for best-dressed goes to . . .Christians." They are dressed in the righteousness of Christ. Their award is heaven itself.

I hope these lines make you stop and think about how you appear—and not how you appear to your friends but how you appear to God. It is also a good idea for you to begin thinking about how you will be clothed when you stand before God in judgment.

Those who, by faith, are clothed in the righteousness of Christ take as their own these words:

I will greatly rejoice in the LORD,
My soul shall be joyful in myGod;
For He has clothed me with the garments of salvation,
He has covered me with the robe of righteousness,
As a bridegroom decks himself with ornaments,
And as a bride adorns herself with her jewels.
(Isa. 61:10)

January 11

Vacationing in a Cemetery

From God's Word, the Bible...

Behold, I tell you a mystery: We shall not all sleep, but we shall all be changed—in a moment, in the twinkling of an eye, at the last trumpet. For the trumpet will sound, and the dead will be raised incorruptible, and we shall be changed. For this corruptible must put on incorruption, and this mortal must put on immortality. So when this corruptible has put on incorruption, and this mortal has put on immortality, then shall be brought to pass the saying that is written: "Death is swallowed up in victory."

From 1 Corinthians 15:50-58

In the fall some years ago, my wife and I did something we had dreamed about for years: we took in the beauty of the northeast. We enjoyed seeing Niagara Falls and the breathtaking foliage of New York, New Hampshire, and Vermont. We also enjoyed visiting the church in Northampton, Massachusetts, where the great theologian Jonathan Edwards served as pastor.

Oddly enough, the highlight of the trip for me was a cemetery in Arlington, Vermont, where we had journeyed to see the Norman Rockwell museum.

The cemetery was very old, with some graves dating back to the late 1700s. One of the gravestones immediately caught my attention. It marked the resting place of a Daniel Ellsworth, who died February 25, 1832, at the age of fifty. I was glad to read these words on the marker:

Thus saith the Comforter,
Earth has no sorrows
Which Heaven cannot heal.

Another stone marked the grave of Samuel Ellsworth, who died July 18, 1819, at the age of 65. At the bottom of this marker was this verse of Scripture: "And what I say unto you I say unto all, 'Watch.'" (Mark 13:37).

As we toured the cemetery, we found that almost every gravestone had words expressing faith in Christ. The inscription I liked best was at the grave of Captain John Gray, who died at age seventy-nine in 1806:

When Christ appears in yonder Cloud
With all His numerous Throng

This believer then shall rise & sing
And Christ shall be the song.

Still another stone was inscribed with these words:

Friends nor Physicians could not save
My mortal body from the grave;
Nor can the grave confine me here,
When Christ my Savior shall appear.

As I walked away from that cemetery, the words of Hebrews 11:4 came to mind: " . . .he being dead still speaks."

The believers whose graves I visited are still speaking hundreds of years after they died. They must have died with the realization that their gravestones would be read by hundreds and thousands from future generations. They wanted even in death to speak plainly to the living about the brevity of life, the certainty of death, and the urgent need to prepare to meet God. They also wanted to bear witness to the only way to stand acceptably in the presence of God, namely, through faith in the saving work of the Lord Jesus Christ.

Still further, they intended in death to taunt death. Even though death had claimed them, it would not be able to hold them. They went to their graves with the unswerving confidence that the very Christ in whom they trusted would come again from heaven, call their bodies from those graves, reunite those bodies to their souls (which went to be with the Lord at the time of death—2 Cor. 5:8), and personally escort them to share in His eternal glory.

I left that cemetery with gratitude swelling up in my heart for the strong and unwavering testimony of those saints of God. I also left praying that unbelievers who visit there would realize the brevity of this life, the certainty of eternity, and the sufficiency of Jesus Christ to prepare them for eternity.

Who Is Really Relevant?

From God's Word, the Bible...

"Beware of false prophets, who come to you in sheep's clothing, but inwardly they are ravenous wolves. You will know them by their fruits. Do men gather grapes from thornbushes or figs from thistles? Even so, every good tree bears good fruit, but a bad tree bears bad fruit. A good tree cannot bear bad fruit, nor can a bad tree bear good fruit. Every tree that does not bear good fruit is cut down and thrown into the fire. Therefore by their fruits you will know them.

Matthew 7:15-20

Scarcely a week can go by without a piece of mail coming my way about a new church starting up—at least that is the way it seems. It won't be long until there are more churches in my city than there are people to attend them!

These pieces of mail almost invariably promise that the new church will be "relevant," "contemporary," "practical," and "uplifting."

There is no great secret here. The churches that use these words are telling us that they will be offering a message about how to live happily and successfully in this world. They are telling us that they will give people help with their finances, their careers, their families, and their personal relationships. They are telling us that we can come to their services without having to fear that we will hear such words as "sin," "judgment," and "repentance." Those words make people feel bad, and these churches want people to feel good! Still further, these pastors and churches are telling us how they regard pastors and churches that still use such words. They are irrelevant, they say!

So I have been thinking about who is relevant and who isn't. Here is a man who has a dreadful and serious illness. He goes to Doctor A, and this doctor tells him that there is nothing seriously wrong with him, and that he simply needs to have a more positive outlook on life. But our patient has the gnawing sense that something is wrong. So he goes to Doctor B. This doctor runs certain tests. On the basis of those tests he tells this man that he, the doctor, has both bad news and good news. The bad news is that he, the patient, has an illness that is so serious that it will eventually kill him; but the good news is that the illness can be successfully treated.

Which of the two doctors is more relevant for this poor man? Now Doctor A may be a very likable, warm, and personable fellow. He may be very witty, clever, and entertaining. He may even give the man tips on how to handle his finances and career and so on. But he is certainly not relevant because he refuses to take seriously the terrible illness that his patient has. Doctor A may consider himself relevant, but in reality he is horribly irrelevant!

Doctor B, on the other hand, may be somewhat lacking in personal charm. He may not be funny or entertaining at all. He may not have any tips for his patient with regard to other areas of his life. He may even dress in a traditional rather than trendy way! But he is powerfully relevant because he acknowledges the illness of his patient and he treats it!

Like it or not, the Bible is very plain about us. It tells us that we are sinful people who are destined to stand at the Judgment Seat of the God who is infinitely holy.

This life will soon pass, and each one of us will face the awesome realities of judgment and eternity. Pastors and churches are called by God to be physicians of souls. We are called to tell people about the reality of their sin and the certainty of divine judgment and also, thank God, to tell them that there is a cure for sin. If they will flee to the Lord Jesus Christ in true repentance and faith, they can be saved!

So who really is relevant? Is it the pastor who refuses to tell people about their sin and the salvation available in Christ? Or is it the pastor who does? The answer is plain. It is one of the great ironies of our time that many pastors who seem to be relevant are really irrelevant, and many pastors who seem to be irrelevant are relevant!

In these days in which preachers are falling all over themselves to help people live in the here and now, we would do well to ever heed these words from the Lord Jesus Christ: "Do not labor for the food which perishes, but for the food which endures to everlasting life, which the Son of Man will give you, because God the Father has set His seal on Him" (John 6:27).

We would also do well to reflect long and hard on the Bible's warnings to not heal the hurt of people "slightly" and not preach peace when there is no peace (Jer. 6:14; 8:11).

January 13

The Epitaph Every Christian Should Desire

From God's Word, the Bible...

And Jehoiada the priest gave to the captains of hundreds the spears and the large and small shields which had belonged to King David, that were in the temple of God. Then he set all the people, every man with his weapon in his hand, from the right side of the temple to the left side of the temple, along by the altar and by the temple, all around the king. And they brought out the king's son, put the crown on him, gave him the Testimony, and made him king. Then Jehoiada and his sons anointed him, and said, "Long live the king!"

From 2 Chronicles 23:1-11

Mel Blanc's gravestone has these words: "That's all folks." Merv Griffin's reads: "I will not be right back after this message."

A lesser-known epitaph is found on the gravestone of one Lester Moore:

Here lies Lester Moore,
Four slugs from a 44.
No less, no more.

Epitaphs don't have to be written on tombstones. They can be any phrase or statement written or spoken in memory of a person who has died.

It is inevitable that others will have something to say about us when we die. Perhaps they will say: "He was a good family man," or "She was a good wife and mother." Perhaps someone will say: "He had a great sense of humor."

What people say of us after we have died will be determined by how we live. Each one of us is now writing a script that will be read when we die. Every Christian should be trying to live in such a way that others, upon his or her death, will have to say the very same thing that the author of 2 Chronicles said of Jehoiada: he (or she) did good "toward God and His house."

Jehoiada is not one of the best-known characters of the Old Testament. That is a shame. He was a great man indeed. When Queen Athaliah was working feverishly to obliterate all the descendants of David, Jehoiada and his wife hid the infant Joash until he was old enough to serve as king At that time Jehoiada put together a plan to put Joash on the throne. It was a plan that worked perfectly. So Jehoiada stood for God in a very evil time and when there were many who stood against God. Jehoiada also believed God's Word even when it seemed absurd to do so. God had promised that David's line would last. With that line down to a single child, there seemed to be little chance of that promise being fulfilled. But Jehoiada continued to believe in that promise, and he believed that God could use him to make the fulfillment a reality.

Jehoiada is still doing good. He rises from the pages of Scripture to urge us to stand for God and to believe His Word. Even in difficult times? Yes!

We should be like Jehoiada. We should earnestly desire to do good toward God for one simple reason: He has done good toward us! If we only had adequate discernment, we could each list a thousand good things that we have received from God. All Christians would put at the top of that list the greatest of all good things—the good thing God did for us when He saved us from our sins and from the eternal destruction those sins deserve.

The way God did this good thing for us was, of course, through the redeeming work of His Son, the Lord Jesus Christ. Perhaps the greatest good we can get from Jehoiada the priest is to look past him to a greater priest who did greater good. That priest is Jesus; that good is salvation for sinners.

We should also fervently desire to do good toward God's house for the same reason—it has done good for us. How often we have come to it with weary, aching hearts only to find that the Lord met us there, opened His Word to us, and encouraged us!

We owe both God and His house a debt that we can never pay, but we can be making payments! We can live for God. We can always speak His name with reverence. We can obey His commandments. We can seek Him in prayer. We can exalt Him in worship. We can be faithful to attend church. We can protect the unity of the church. We can support the mission of the church. And we can pray for the success of the church. While others only live to do good for themselves, let us determine that we will be Jehoiadas who do good toward God and His church.

A Little Skimping

FROM GOD'S WORD, THE BIBLE...

I have rejoiced in the way of Your testimonies,
As much as in all riches.
I will meditate on Your precepts,
And contemplate Your ways.
I will delight myself in Your statutes;
I will not forget Your word.

Your testimonies are wonderful;
Therefore my soul keeps them.
The entrance of Your words gives light;
It gives understanding to the simple.
I opened my mouth and panted,
For I longed for Your commandments.

PSALM 119:14-16; 129-131

Years ago I saw an amusing yet thought-provoking cartoon depicting two stone masons with trowels in hand walking away from a sign that read "Future site of the Tower of Pisa." One of them was saying: "I skimped a little on the foundation, but no one will ever know the difference."

A little skimping here and there can make a huge difference.

Just as we receive physical life through physical birth so we receive spiritual life through spiritual birth (John 1:12-13; 3:1-8).

Babies are adorable, but parents do not want their children to remain babies. They want them to grow. So it is in the spiritual realm. We come into it as spiritual babies, but God doesn't want us to remain babies. He wants us to grow.

The Word of God is the primary means that God has appointed for our spiritual growth. It is to us, spiritually, what food is to us, physically. The Apostle Peter urged his readers to "desire the pure milk of the word" so that they could "grow thereby" (1 Peter 2:2).

Nothing is more important to our spiritual health than the intake of the Word of God. We are to do this privately by reading it, studying it, reading about it, discussing it, and reflecting on it. And we are to do it publicly. We are to gather with our brothers and sisters in Christ in a church that accurately preaches and teaches the Word of God. As it is preached and taught, we are to give our full attention to it. J.I. Packer was right to make this point:

Congregations never honor God more than by reverently listening to His Word. . .

But what if we begin to "skimp a little"? Yes, what then? What if we decide to cut back in our worship attendance? We may think that it will not hurt us spiritually, but sustained absence from God's Word will prove detrimental to our spiritual health, just as sustained absence from eating will prove detrimental to our physical health.

Sadly enough, churches and pastors are promoting the skimping mentality by greatly reducing the number of opportunities for people to hear the preaching of God's Word. My wife and I grew up in an era in which there were a great many opportunities to hear God's Word. There was preaching on Sunday morning and Sunday evening and teaching in a midweek service (and these services were never cancelled during holidays). And our country churches had "revival services." These were two-week events that were conducted in the spring and the fall, and, yes, there was preaching every night. We (my wife and I) estimate that, barring illness, we were in a hundred-and-fifty preaching services a year. Many churches these days would be challenged to offer fifty such services. Is this skimping hurting us? I believe it is. We are living in very dark and critical times. We need answers. The Bible alone contains the answers we need. It tells us why we are the way we are and what God has done in and through His Son, Jesus Christ, to change us. We need more of the Bible, not less. We need it in large doses, and it is hard to get those doses in this era of skimping.

January 15

Why This Waste?

From God's Word, the Bible...

And when Jesus was in Bethany at the house of Simon the leper, a woman came to Him having an alabaster flask of very costly fragrant oil, and she poured it on His head as He sat at the table. But when His disciples saw it, they were indignant, saying, "Why this waste? For this fragrant oil might have been sold for much and given to the poor."
But when Jesus was aware of it, He said to them, "Why do you trouble the woman? For she has done a good work for Me. For you have the poor with you always, but Me you do not have always. For in pouring this fragrant oil on My body, she did it for My burial. Assuredly, I say to you, wherever this gospel is preached in the whole world, what this woman has done will also be told as a memorial to her."

Matthew 26:6-13

The disciples could scarcely believe their eyes. While they and Jesus were enjoying supper at the house of Simon the leper (evidently this was Simon's expression of gratitude to Jesus for healing him of his leprosy), a woman came to Jesus, broke open a box of very costly oil, and poured it out on His head.

Filled with indignation, the disciples pounced on the poor woman. "Why this waste?" was their stern question (Matt. 26:8).

This was foolish, extravagant, and senseless, they inferred. The poor could have certainly used the money that would have been realized had the ointment been sold. What this woman had done was, therefore, tantamount to taking food out of the mouths of the poor.

This outburst represented an aberration for the disciples. They certainly did not believe that anything done for Jesus would be a waste. But there are those who do so believe. What was a momentary glitch for the disciples is a settled mentality with many people these days. They look at the church and pronounce it all a waste—a waste of time, energy, and money. To them it is all so foolish and senseless. Those who give themselves to the Lord's work are frequently considered to be rather pathetic souls who could, were it not for their lack of enlightenment, be giving themselves to things that really matter. When they see Christians doing anything in the name of Christ, they eagerly resurrect the disciples' question: "Why this waste?"

These critics would have said the same when some of David's men did an extraordinary thing to get David a drink from Bethlehem's well. You remember the story. David was a fugitive, hiding in the cave of Adullam from the murderous rage of King Saul. And Bethlehem, his beloved home, was now in the hands of the Philistines.

Difficulties and hardships have a way of making us yearn for easier, simpler times. We are not surprised, then, that there in the cave David was thinking about his childhood years.

One of the pleasures of summertime was coming to Bethlehem while bathed in sweat and covered in grime and drawing a cool, refreshing drink from the well at the gate.

As David pondered that happier time, these words suddenly slipped out: "Oh, that someone would give me a drink of water from the well of Bethlehem, which is by the gate" (2 Sam. 23:15).

Caught up in that moment of nostalgia, David may very well not have even heard himself say those words. But others heard him. Three of his "mighty men" took the bare expression of that wish so very seriously that they broke through the Philistine lines, drew water from the well of Bethlehem, and brought it to David (2 Sam. 23:16).

What drove these men to do this? It was love for their captain, love so deep and strong that they regarded his mere wish as their duty, and, yes, their highest privilege. Some would call what they did foolhardy, but it made perfect sense to David's men. They loved their captain so much that they were willing to "waste" time and energy to please him.

And it was love for the Lord Jesus that drove Mary to "waste" her ointment. She had been enabled to foresee Jesus' saving work on the cross. The disciples had undoubtedly congratulated themselves on being terribly perceptive about her act, but this woman they belittled far outpaced them in perception. Her anointing of Jesus flowed from nothing less than a heart amazed at the thought of Calvary's love.

She looked down the corridor of days
Saw Calvary's love and stood amazed.
She saw that dying form, that disfigured face,
And marveled at the sight of redeeming grace.

Those who understand the cross of Christ and marvel at God's redeeming grace are ready to respond to the skeptics. With hearts full of love, we emphatically say: It is no waste to pour out the ointment of our lives in the worship and service of Jesus Christ. Through Him we have been rescued from condemnation and made heirs of eternal life. He is our glorious Savior. It is not a waste to serve Him. It is rather a waste not to serve Him. Going back to David's men for a moment, we must say that Christ, the captain of our salvation (Heb. 2:10), is far greater than David ever was. He is worthy of greater devotion than David's men showed him.

The Dying Thief Rejoiced to See That Fountain in His Day

From God's Word, the Bible...

Then one of the criminals who were hanged blasphemed Him, saying, "If You are the Christ, save Yourself and us." But the other, answering, rebuked him, saying, "Do you not even fear God, seeing you are under the same condemnation? And we indeed justly, for we receive the due reward of our deeds; but this Man has done nothing wrong." Then he said to Jesus, "Lord, remember me when You come into Your kingdom." And Jesus said to him, "Assuredly, I say to you, today you will be with Me in Paradise."

Luke 23:39-43

There is a fountain filled with blood, Drawn from Immanuel's veins,
And sinners plunged beneath that flood, Lose all their guilty stains.
The dying thief rejoiced to see, That fountain in His day;
And there may I, though vile as he, Wash all my sins away.

(There is a Fountain, William Cowper, 1772)

One of the greatest joys of heaven will be meeting all the interesting people who will be there. I am looking forward to meeting the thief to whom William Cowper referred when he wrote these words.

This is the thief of Luke 23:39-43. It is the thief who, after initially heaping scorn and mockery on Jesus, cried to Him: "Lord remember me when you come into Your kingdom."

It is the thief who heard these enormously cheering words from Jesus: "Today you will be with Me in paradise."

But doesn't a "fountain filled with blood" sound strange? Cowper chose his words carefully, basing them squarely on this promise: "In that day a fountain shall be opened for the house of David and for the inhabitants of Jerusalem, for sin and for uncleanness" (Zech. 13:1). We know a fountain is a device that sends out a stream of water. We associate it with a constant and abundant supply of water. Cowper was affirming that Jesus' death on the cross opened a constant and abundant supply of cleansing for sinners.

How does the blood of Jesus cleanse sinners? The blood is shorthand for the death of the Lord Jesus, and death in all its forms (physical, spiritual, eternal) is the penalty for sin. On the cross Jesus took that penalty so all who trust in Him will never have to bear it themselves.

The thief "rejoiced" to see that fountain. He was about to go out into eternity laden down with his many violations of God's laws. His case would seem to be hopeless. But the grace of God enabled him to understand that the man next to him was no ordinary man dying an ordinary death. He was there as the King of an eternal kingdom, and He was dying so that even the vilest of sinners could be part of that kingdom. All that was necessary was for this thief to cry out to this King, and cry he did.

The fountain He opened on the cross is still flowing. It cleanses all sinners who cry out to Christ in repentance and faith. Even great sinners? Yes, even great sinners!

John Newton certainly fell into the category of a great sinner. Slave trader, drunkard, brawler, blasphemer—Newton was all that and more. But he found the Lord, or, more accurately, the Lord found him. Are you thinking that the name John Newton sounds familiar? It should. He is the author of the much-loved and much-sung *Amazing Grace*:

Amazing grace! how sweet the sound, That saved a wretch like me!
I once was lost, but now am found, Was blind, but now I see.

When Newton lay dying his friend John Jay came to visit him. Jay leaned over him and asked: "John, do you know me?" Newton replied: "I only know two things. I am a great sinner, and Jesus is a great Savior."

One of the most beautiful sights of heaven will be seeing the repentant thief standing alongside Newton—both great sinners, both saved by grace. We may even hear the thief say to Newton: "John, let's sing that song you wrote once again." If I do happen to hear him say that, I will gladly join in, singing most heartily:

How precious did that grace appear
The hour I first believed!

But the truth of the matter is that we are all great sinners. Paul writes: "There is none righteous, no, not one" (Rom. 3:10). So we all need to turn to Christ as this thief did.

While we rejoice over the conversion of this thief, we should never forget that there was another thief who did not repent. It was not mere coincidence that Jesus' cross was placed between the crosses of the two thieves. He is ever the great divider of men. Those who receive Him are saved; those who reject Him are forever lost. Nothing is of greater importance than making sure we are in the company of the believing thief and not in the company of the other.

January 17

Why Does Christianity Seem to Mean so Little to so Many?

From God's Word, the Bible...

"Therefore whoever hears these sayings of Mine, and does them, I will liken him to a wise man who built his house on the rock: and the rain descended, the floods came, and the winds blew and beat on that house; and it did not fall, for it was founded on the rock.
. . .But everyone who hears these sayings of Mine, and does not do them, will be like a foolish man who built his house on the sand: and the rain descended, the floods came, and the winds blew and beat on that house; and it fell. And great was its fall."

From Matthew 7:21-29

Having served as a pastor for many years, I have come to this disconcerting conclusion: Christianity doesn't mean much to a lot of people who regard themselves as Christians.

Christians believe that they have been delivered from God's just punishment for their sins—eternal destruction in hell—because Jesus Christ endured their hell when He died on the cross. By virtue of the Spirit of God operating in their hearts, Christians have repented of their sins and put their trust for eternal salvation in the Lord Jesus and in what He did on their behalf.

There is nothing we can do to earn our salvation, but there are many things we can do to show our gratitude for salvation. Here are a few:

- We can read and study God's Word to discover how He wants us to live, and then live according to the things we discover.
- We can talk to the Lord in prayer, personally expressing to Him our gratitude for what He has done for us and asking Him to help us live for Him.
- We can worship Him in His house on a weekly basis (which, by the way, is one of His commandments).
- We can generously give money to support the Lord's work. Tithing is a good place to start!
- We can show love and appreciation to those whom God has sent to help us live for Him. (And, yes, I'm referring to pastors!)

These and the other things that God requires of us would seem to be the very least Christians can do to express their gratitude to God for graciously delivering them from hell. One would think every Christian would gladly do all that God asks and then say: "What more can I do?" After all, being delivered from hell is no small thing!

But, amazingly enough, many people who profess to be Christians find these things to be too much for them. They never read their Bibles or pray. They never, or very rarely, attend church services. They give little or nothing to the Lord's work. They do not pray for their pastors or come to hear their preaching and teaching. They say they are Christians, but they feel no gratitude. They say they are saved, but they do not feel indebted. They say their hell has been replaced with heaven, but they do not feel obligated to do anything for God.

So church leaders find themselves confronted with this question: Why does Christianity seem to mean very little or nothing to these people who claim to be Christians?

There are two answers. The first is that it is possible for true Christians to allow themselves to get into such a terribly cold and backslidden condition that, for a while, they do not live as they should.

While backsliding is indeed prevalent, I think the second answer is more often the explanation—that many of these people are simply not Christians at all! They think they are, but they are not! They believe they have been delivered from hell, but every day off the calendar moves them one step closer to it. Becoming a Christian is not a matter of walking an aisle, being baptized, and getting one's name in a church book. It is a matter of having so encountered the living God that one's life is changed. If there is no change, there is no Christianity! It is as simple and as frightening as that!

The sad truth is many expect their so-called Christianity to get them to heaven, and yet it won't even get them to church! These poor people will not realize their true state until that day they expect to enter heaven only to hear the Lord Jesus say: "I never knew you; depart from Me. . ." (Matt. 7:23).

All of Christianity can be boiled down to three words: GUILT, GRACE, and GRATITUDE. All of us have the guilt—the guilt of sin. But only Christians have the grace and the gratitude. All Christians have received God's grace in salvation, and all express their gratitude. If there is no gratitude, it is because there is no grace!

What to Preach on at Easter

From God's Word, the Bible...

"Because I live, you will live also. At that day you will know that I am in My Father, and you in Me, and I in you."
Now Jesus knew that they desired to ask Him, and He said to them, "Are you inquiring among yourselves about what I said, 'A little while, and you will not see Me; and again a little while, and you will see Me'? Most assuredly, I say to you that you will weep and lament, but the world will rejoice; and you will be sorrowful, but your sorrow will be turned into joy. A woman, when she is in labor, has sorrow because her hour has come; but as soon as she has given birth to the child, she no longer remembers the anguish, for joy that a human being has been born into the world. Therefore you now have sorrow; but I will see you again and your heart will rejoice, and your joy no one will take from you."

From John 14:19,20; John 16:16-22

Several years ago, a distraught woman asked if she could talk with me about a matter that was weighing heavily on her mind and heart. A member of a mega-church, she was troubled by what she heard her pastor say on Easter Sunday. With thousands present, he began his message with these words:

"I realize it is Easter, and you all are expecting to hear a sermon about the resurrection, but I want to preach on something more relevant." He then proceeded to deliver a message about modern-day family living!

I assured her that she was right to be troubled. If we were all destined to continue to live on this earth the same kind of lives that we are living now, a message on some aspect of life in this world would be very relevant indeed. But, there's the rub! Our lives on this earth do not stretch out endlessly! They have an end to them. We all have an appointment with death (Heb. 9:27).

I certainly have nothing against a preacher talking about the importance of the family or some other aspect of living in this world. Such subjects must be addressed because the Bible itself addresses them. The problem is that many preachers these days are talking *exclusively* about such topics. To hear them preach, one would never get the impression that death is racing toward us and eternity is opening its arms to receive us.

Because death is always the greatest fact of life, I am not in a dilemma about what I will preach on Easter. The resurrection of Jesus will be my theme!

What relevance does the resurrection of Jesus have for dying people? Much! By His resurrection, Jesus proved Himself to be exactly what He claimed to be—God in human flesh (Rom. 1:4). If He is God, He cannot lie (Num. 23:19; Titus 1:2). If He cannot lie, the words He spoke to Martha must come true: "I am the resurrection and the life. He who believes in Me, though he may die, he shall live" (John 11:25).

Because Jesus arose from the grave, those who believe in Him as their Lord and Savior do not have to worry about death. It will not have the final word regarding them. The Lord Jesus will raise their bodies from their graves (1 Thess. 4:14-16) and give them bodies fashioned after His own resurrection body (Phil. 3:20-21).

His victory over death guarantees their victory over death. He Himself says to all His people: "Because I live, you will live also" (John 14:19). The Apostle Paul assured the Christians in Rome of this truth by writing: "He who raised Christ from the dead will also give life to your mortal bodies through the Spirit who dwells in you" (Rom. 8:11).

Thomas Watson, one of the Puritans, triumphantly affirmed the resurrection of God's people in these memorable words: "We are more sure to rise out of our grave than out of our beds."

Something more relevant than the resurrection of Jesus? I think not! As a dying man, I will again next Easter look to the resurrection of Jesus as my hope and my joy. If the resurrection of Jesus is irrelevant, let me be irrelevant this Easter and every other day!

What about Hypocrites in the Church?

From God's Word, the Bible...

And you know that He was manifested to take away our sins, and in Him there is no sin.

1 John 3:5

Our English word "hypocrite" comes from the Greek word "hupokrites." That word was used for Greek and Roman actors who covered their faces and distorted their voices so that they appeared to be someone other than themselves.

These actors had two faces. One was the face behind the mask, and the other was the face of the mask. The two were, of course, quite different.

From that simple beginning the word came to be applied to anyone who pretends to be something he is not. The person himself is one way, but he holds up a mask, as it were, to hide the reality and to give the impression that he is someone quite different.

Jesus charged the Pharisees with hypocrisy. They wanted to give the impression that they loved God, but Jesus knew there was no real love for God in them but only love for themselves.

No charge is more frequently leveled against Christians today than that of hypocrisy, and many unbelievers use the hypocrisy of believers, whether perceived or real, as their reason for rejecting Christ.

This is, then, an issue that we cannot ignore. How should Christians respond to the issue of hypocrisy?

We must first point out the simple truth that not all are Christians who claim to be. The fact that one *professes* faith in Christ does not mean that he actually *possesses* faith in Christ.

We should always remember that the Bible gives several warnings about the matter of being deceived (Matt. 7:21-23; 2 Cor. 13:5; 2 Peter 1:10) as well as examples of men who were deceived about their faith (Judas, Demas). The Bible also gives us certain tests we can use to determine if we are truly saved (1 John). All of this would be pointless unless it is terribly possible to think we are saved when we are not.

In the second place, we must point out that the Bible's teaching about Christians is far different than the popular understanding of Christians. In other words, people who accuse Christians of hypocrisy often employ a higher standard for Christian behavior than does the Bible.

The Bible teaches that conversion makes a profound and lasting change in the individual, but it does not teach that the Christian will ever attain perfection in this life. To the contrary, the Bible teaches the reality of indwelling sin in the life of the Christian and the ongoing conflict the Christian has with sin.

The Christian will never be completely free from sin in this life. He is a work in progress. He has been forgiven of his sins and made right with God (an act of God called *justification*). He is now growing and maturing (a process called *sanctification*). He will finally be freed from sin and made like Christ (an event called *glorification*).

Someone put it like this: "I am not what I ought to be. I am not what I am going to be. But, thank God, I am not what I used to be."

When unbelievers see evidence of imperfection in the Christian, they are seeing the truth of the Bible confirmed!

By the way, Jesus Himself clearly indicated that hypocrites would be found wherever true faith is found (Matt. 24:11,24), and, as noted above, even had a hypocrite among His disciples.

In the third place, we should point out that all hypocrites will finally be exposed and judged.

Every Christian is hypocritical to some extent because no Christian is perfect. But those who, on the one hand, continually show themselves to be hypocrites and, on the other hand, are never troubled by their failures, never repent, and never give any evidence of genuine faith will experience the fulfillment of the Lord's promise of judgment (Luke 12:1-5).

Finally, we must always be eager to say that the Lord Jesus Christ was not a hypocrite.

The question each unbeliever must face is not whether Christians are hypocrites, but whether Jesus was a hypocrite. We are not saved by other Christians; we are saved by Jesus!

Those who closely study the life of Jesus find no evidence of failure or sin in Him but rather find themselves taking as their own the words of Pontius Pilate, who said of Jesus: "I find no fault in Him" (John 19:6).

Finding God's Will

From God's Word, the Bible...

Trust in the Lord with all your heart,
And lean not on your own understanding;
In all your ways acknowledge Him,
And He shall direct your paths.

Proverbs 3:5, 6

Christians know several things about this matter of finding and understanding the will of God:

- God has a will for their lives—that is, He does care how they live.
- He does not merely shrug and say: "Do what you want." God's will is right and good. Christians fully subscribe to Paul's teaching that the will of God is "good and acceptable and perfect" (Rom. 12:2).
- They must eventually stand before God and give account of the way in which they lived (Rom. 14:12). Those who live most completely in line with the will of God will be much more at peace on that day.

The main problems Christians face on the matter of the will of God are discovering it and carrying it out. This devotional reading is designed to help with the first of these problems.

How can we know the will of God for our lives? The first thing for us to do probably sounds strange. We must relax! We have a tendency to think that discovering the will of God depends entirely on us, but the truth is that the Lord leads His children far more than they realize (Ps. 23:1-3; 32:8; 37:23; Rom. 8:14; Phil. 2:13).

The second thing for us to do is read and study the Bible.

- The Bible lays out God's purpose for each of His children, namely, living in such a way as to bring honor to Him (1 Peter 2:9-10).
- The Bible gives us direct commandments and prohibitions (e.g., The Ten Commandments).
- The Bible gives us a pattern to follow (Phil. 2:5-11).
- The Bible and the Holy Spirit always agree.

The third thing for us to do is refocus. If we primarily focus our attention on being the right kind of people and on performing the duties that God has assigned to us, the will of God will find us.

Proverbs 3:5-6 teaches us to occupy ourselves with trusting in the Lord and acknowledging Him in all our ways. If we will do these things, we can be assured that the Lord will direct our paths.

Adrian Rogers captured this truth in these words: "The will of God is not a *road map*; it is a *relationship*. . ."

What is the outcome of acknowledging God in all our ways? Charles Bridges says: "No step well prayed over will bring ultimate regret. Though the promise will not rend us infallible; our very error will be overruled for deeper humiliation and self-knowledge; and thus even this mysterious direction will in the end be gratefully acknowledged, 'He led me forth in the right way.'" (Ps. 107:7).

The final thing for us to do is ask. The Bible assures us that God will grant us wisdom if we will ask Him for it (James 1:5).

In praying about the will of God, we should also hold before God His promises to guide His people, as the hymn-writer did in these lines:

I need Thee every hour, most gracious Lord;
No tender voice like Thine can peace afford.
I need Thee every hour, teach me Thy will;
Thy promise so rich in me fulfill.

Here are some other guidelines that will help us on this matter of finding God's will:

- If we want to know more of the will of God, we must practice those things which we already know to be His will. God is not obligated to reveal more of His will to those who are disregarding that which He has already revealed.
- We must be careful about assuming how God will lead—that is, we must not think that God's will is always the most unpleasant course of action. God gives us certain desires and inclinations and then works through those desires. On the other hand, we must not as-sume that the will of God is easy and problem free.
- Consult circumstances, spiritual leaders, and spiritual friends.
- Be patient. We tend to be great believers in instant gratification, but God does not work according to our schedules.

January 21

How Can We Be Sure God Exists?

FROM GOD'S WORD, THE BIBLE...

"If you had known Me, you would have known My Father also; and from now on you know Him and have seen Him." Philip said to Him, "Lord, show us the Father, and it is sufficient for us." Jesus said to him, "Have I been with you so long, and yet you have not known Me, Philip? He who has seen Me has seen the Father; so how can you say, 'Show us the Father'? Do you not believe that I am in the Father, and the Father in Me? The words that I speak to you I do not speak on My own authority; but the Father who dwells in Me does the works. Believe Me that I am in the Father and the Father in Me, or else believe Me for the sake of the works themselves.

JOHN 14:7-11

There is no need to belabor the importance of this question. Everyone is agreed on its importance. If God exists, this world is one kind of world; if He does not, it is a radically different kind. If God exists, we are one kind of being; if He does not, we are a far different kind. If God exists, we are required to live one kind of life; if He does not, we can live an entirely different kind. If God exists, we have one kind of future; if He does not, we have a totally different kind.

The question, then, is not the importance of the question! It is rather how we can know for sure that God exists.

It is interesting that the Bible does not argue for the existence of God but assumes it (Gen. 1:1). It does not debate with the atheist, but rather dismisses such a person (Ps. 14:1).

This dismissal is not due to a lack of evidence for God but rather to such an abundance of evidence that the atheist does not have a leg on which to stand. God has not left Himself without witness! (See Acts 14:17.)

The created order itself gives powerful testimony to God (Ps. 19:1-6; Acts 14:15-16; Rom. 1:18-20).

Don Fortner has rightly observed: "Three things are revealed to all men in creation which cannot be denied. The Book of God declares that all men know these three things about God; (1) God is (2) God is wise (3) God is almighty."

The witness of the created order to God compelled Abraham Lincoln to say: "I cannot conceive of how any man could look up into the heavens and say there is no God."

God has also left witness to Himself by giving each individual an intuitive knowledge that He, God, exists, that we are His creatures and must eventually give account of ourselves to Him. The Apostle Paul tells us that this knowledge is so powerful that the only way it can be silenced is for men to "suppress" it (Rom. 1:18-19). The word "suppress" suggests putting the truth in a box and nailing the lid shut!

The outer testimony of creation and the inner testimony of conscience are compelling and persuasive, but the most definitive proof of God is Christ.

The Lord Jesus Christ claimed to be God in human flesh (John 14:7-11). He claimed to be sent by God (John 7:28-29; 8:42), to exercise the prerogatives of God (John 5:21-23,25-27), to do the works of God (John 10:37-38) and to speak for God (John 12:49-50).

The Apostle John, who was closely associated with Jesus for more than three years, also affirmed that He was God (John 1:14,18; 1 John 1:1-2).

The miracles of Jesus prove that He was God. These miracles were great in number, were of all types, and were witnessed by multitudes.

The teachings of Jesus indicated that He was God (Matt. 7:28-29; 13:54; John 7:46).

The many prophecies He fulfilled give us yet another proof of Jesus' deity, and His resurrection from the dead is the towering, crowning proof that He was God (Rom. 1:4).

Here is the point: if Jesus was God, God exists!

All the proofs for the existence of God, powerful and persuasive as they are, will not convince people of the existence of God. They may help us to win the argument, but they will not help us to win the sinner (1 Cor. 2:14). That work can only be accomplished by the Holy Spirit of God. The Apostle Paul declares: ". . .no one can say that Jesus is Lord except by the Holy Spirit" (1 Cor. 12:3).

We must recognize that people do not disbelieve in God because they have intellectual problems that they cannot resolve, but because they have a spiritual problem they won't face. They don't believe in God because they don't want there to be a God. Only the Spirit of God can change their hearts.

We Christians have another problem. Because the Spirit of God has worked in our hearts, we do not need to be convinced of the existence of God. Our need is to feel passion for the God whose existence we acknowledge—to feel such passion that we will live for His glory.

Just Call Me Barabbas

From God's Word, the Bible...

And they all cried out at once, saying, "Away with this Man, and release to us Barabbas"—who had been thrown into prison for a certain rebellion made in the city, and for murder.
Pilate, therefore, wishing to release Jesus, again called out to them. But they shouted, saying, "Crucify Him, crucify Him!"
Then he said to them the third time, "Why, what evil has He done? I have found no reason for death in Him. I will therefore chastise Him and let Him go." But they were insistent, demanding with loud voices that He be crucified. And the voices of these men and of the chief priests prevailed. So Pilate gave sentence that it should be as they requested. And he released to them the one they requested, who for rebellion and murder had been thrown into prison; but he delivered Jesus to their will.

From Luke 23:13-25

Barabbas was a dead man, and Pilate was a desperate man. I say Barabbas was a dead man because he had been condemned to die. He was found guilty of insurrection and murder. The sentence had been handed down and only a few dreary hours were lying between Barabbas and the execution of that sentence.

Pilate, on the other hand, was a desperate man. The Jewish leaders were demanding that Jesus be crucified, and Pilate knew that Jesus had done nothing to deserve such a fate. So Pilate was in a dilemma and desperate to get out of it.

But Pilate was also a clever man. He would give the Jews a choice! He would bring both Jesus and Barabbas before the people and let them decide who would be released and who would be crucified.

As far as Pilate was concerned, it was a no-brainer. The people would choose Jesus, the man who had gone about healing the sick, casting out demons, and proclaiming the kingdom of God. Barabbas, on the other hand, was such a low-life character that all would be glad to be rid of him.

It was perfect! Barabbas the guilty would receive the death he deserved, and Jesus the innocent would go free.

After many hours of tossing and turning, Barabbas finally falls asleep. But suddenly he is awakened by the clanking of armor and the loud talking of Roman soldiers. They are on their way to get him, and he is on his way to the cross!

But much to his surprise, Barabbas finds himself being escorted to Pilate's hall. What is going on? Barabbas soon has his answer. He is standing on a balcony with Pilate and a man named Jesus, and Pilate is asking the large throng below to choose whether he, Barabbas, or Jesus should be released!

There is no doubt in Barabbas' mind on how this is going to turn out! The multitude will choose Jesus, and he will keep his appointment with the cross. The only thing this would change is the time. He will be crucified a bit later but still crucified.

Now to his amazement he hears the crowd crying, "We want Barabbas!" And Pilate, equally astonished, asks: "What shall I do with Jesus?" And the crowd angrily shouts: "Crucify Him! Crucify Him!"

Pilate turns to a soldier and says: "Release Barabbas and prepare Jesus for crucifixion."

Barabbas is not quite sure what to do with himself. He finally decides to follow the crowd out to Golgotha. And now they are hoisting the cross on which Jesus had been nailed, and Barabbas says to himself: "I would have been there had Jesus not been put in my place."

My name is Barabbas. As he was guilty of breaking the laws of the Roman government, I stand guilty of breaking God's laws. As he was justly condemned to physical death, I have been justly condemned to eternal death. But as Barabbas' place on the cross was taken by Jesus, so my place was taken by Jesus. Yes, my name is Barabbas. Jesus died in my place, receiving the eternal wrath I deserve. And now there is no penalty left for me to pay. Oh, my heart, rejoice!

A Crisis of Faith

From God's Word, the Bible...

"I do not receive honor from men. But I know you, that you do not have the love of God in you. I have come in My Father's name, and you do not receive Me; if another comes in his own name, him you will receive. How can you believe, who receive honor from one another, and do not seek the honor that comes from the only God? Do not think that I shall accuse you to the Father; there is one who accuses you—Moses, in whom you trust. For if you believed Moses, you would believe Me; for he wrote about Me. But if you do not believe his writings, how will you believe My words?"

From John 5:31-47

Several years ago I experienced a crisis of faith that was so severe that I was not sure whether I could continue to embrace Christianity. I look back at that time now with embarrassment. I thought at the time that my faith was something that I was holding, and I wasn't sure whether I could keep my grip. Now I realize that it was my faith that was holding me.

The one issue that held me was the Gospel accounts of the life and ministry of Jesus. I could not get around the evidence for Him. I found Him inescapably to be the Christ. The only conclusion that made sense to me was that He was God in human flesh. His miraculous deeds and His powerful and astounding teachings, all of which were substantiated by numerous witnesses, left me no room to maneuver. I had tried to get away from Him, but He pursued and conquered me.

I still do not have all the answers that I would like. I am not a Christian because Christianity answers all my questions. I am a Christian because Christianity gives me answers that I cannot get around. Somewhere along life's journey, it occurred to me that the truth about Jesus is so strong and compelling that I could safely put my questions in my hip pocket until I enter heaven's glory. There in His presence, I expect to finally get them answered, and I expect to find that the answers will all make perfect sense. I also expect to feel no little embarrassment over allowing such things to trouble me.

I recall that Nathanael originally thought he could not accept Jesus as the Messiah because Jesus was from Nazareth, but at Philip's insistence, he, Nathanael, agreed to see Jesus. When Jesus told him that He had seen him under the fig tree before Philip ever spoke to him, Nathanael realized the truth. Jesus was indeed the Messiah (John 1:43-51). It's interesting to me that

Nathanael accepted Jesus as the Messiah without ever getting his Nazareth problem resolved. The evidence for Jesus overwhelmed Nathanael. He realized that he could wait to get his Nazareth question answered. He could not wait to confess the truth about Jesus.

Like Nathanael, I have my Nazareth issues, but the evidence for Jesus overwhelms them—and me! The miracles He performed, the words that He spoke, the lives that He changed, the prophecies He fulfilled, and His resurrection all tell me that He was God in human flesh and that He is worthy of my love and devotion. It is not merely that I choose to believe in Jesus. It is rather that I must believe in Him.

I trust that, by the grace of God, I have learned to believe my beliefs and doubt my doubts. I believe in Jesus. I believe that He, the second Person of the Trinity, came to this earth in our humanity. I believe that He died a special kind of death, one such as no one before or since has died. I believe that on the cross He received the wrath of God in my stead so that I will never have to experience that wrath myself. I believe that He arose from the dead and lives today to make intercession for His people. I believe that He gave the Holy Spirit to His people to guide, comfort, strengthen and encourage them. I believe that I will see Him when He comes again and will marvel at the sight of His nail-pierced hands and wounded side. I believe that I will be made like Him and in the ceaseless ages of eternity will be lost in wonder, love and praise.

Yes, I believe in Jesus.

Weird Things

From God's Word, the Bible...

"Do not lay up for yourselves treasures on earth, where moth and rust destroy and where thieves break in and steal; but lay up for yourselves treasures in heaven, where neither moth nor rust destroys and where thieves do not break in and steal. For where your treasure is, there your heart will be also."

Matthew 6:19-21

Do you pay attention to some of the weird things that take place and are reported in the news? I heard a couple of very weird things reported some time ago. One is the story of a man who was so elated that the New York Jets defeated the New England Patriots that he jumped on his sled and went speeding down his icy driveway right out into the street where he was hit by a car and killed! He was so happy over one game that he didn't get to see the next game!

Another news report showed a clip of a young woman who was so engrossed in texting as she walked along that she fell into a pool!

It is not hard to see what these stories have in common. These people were so caught up in the moment that they did not see any danger. Isolated incidents? Not at all! Our nation is filled with people who are very much like the two in these stories. They are so caught up in the here and now that they don't think about the reality and the danger of the Judgment Day that is lying ahead, and they are making no preparation for it.

Another story that comes to my mind is that of the death of Don Meredith, who was fond of wrapping up the games on Monday Night Football with the words, "Turn out the lights, the party's over." Those who are so engaged with the here and now would do well to reflect on those words. Life in this world is coming to an end. The lights will soon be turned out, the party will be over, and it will be time to meet God! How we need to heed these words from Jesus: "Do not labor for the food which perishes, but for the food which endures to everlasting life..." (John 6:27).

Then there is the story of Arthur Stace. Born to alcoholic parents and in deep poverty, Arthur was converted on the night of August 6, 1930, at St. Barnabas Church in Sydney, Australia.

Two years later he heard Reverend John Ridley say: "Eternity, Eternity, I wish that I could sound or shout that word to everyone in the streets of Sydney. You've got to meet it; where will you spend Eternity?"

Arthur would later say: "Eternity went ringing through my brain and suddenly I began crying and felt a powerful call from the Lord to write Eternity."

So write it he did. So night after night he would walk around his city and write the word ETERNITY in chalk wherever he could find a spot. Arthur did not do this for just a week, a month or a year. He stayed with it year after year. It was finally estimated that he wrote that single word in public places at least 500,000 times in thirty-five years.

For a long time, the citizens of Sydney did not know the name of the person who was filling their city with this single word. As they saw it time after time, they must have wondered who was writing it. Finally, a reporter solved the mystery. It was Arthur Stace. From then on, Arthur was called Mr. Eternity.

We can be sure of two things. One is that Arthur Stace lived with the daily awareness of eternity. The other is that he caused many others to be aware of it as well.

Arthur died on July 30, 1967, finally entering into the eternal glory that was so much on his mind in this life.

Some would call him weird, but the truly weird thing is not to live thinking about eternity but rather to live without thinking about it and preparing for it. And the only way to prepare for it is by trusting in the Lord Jesus Christ.

When It Happens

FROM GOD'S WORD, THE BIBLE...

Who among you will give ear to this?
Who will listen and hear for the time to come?
Who gave Jacob for plunder, and Israel to the robbers?
Was it not the LORD,
He against whom we have sinned?
For they would not walk in His ways,
Nor were they obedient to His law.
Therefore He has poured on him the fury of His anger
And the strength of battle;
It has set him on fire all around,
Yet he did not know;
And it burned him,
Yet he did not take it to heart.

ISAIAH 42:23-25

I include myself in the category of the many who think our nation may very well be headed toward unprecedented calamity. I do not know whether that calamity will consist of a terrorist attack, a natural disaster, an epidemic, a complete financial collapse or some combination of these things.

I do know this—if and when such a calamity occurs, many will cry out: "How could God let this happen?"

That, I suggest, will be the wrong question. The right question will be: "How could we let this happen?"

God has placed us in this world and has given us a very definite and distinct assignment. We are to live for His glory. We do this by obeying His commandments. When we live as God commands, we bring blessings into our lives. When we refuse to do so, we invite Him to judge us. In other words, we invite Him to send calamity upon us.

How are we doing with this matter of living in this world as God has commanded? Not well! Consider the following:

- We consistently treat God's name as if it were a light and trivial thing instead of something to be reverenced.
- We consistently use God's day as if it were designed for us to do those things that bring us pleasure. How frequently God's house is forsaken these days for the flimsiest reasons!
- Many who do attend church choose services for their entertainment

value and emotional appeal instead of their commitment to faith-fully expounding the Word of God and declaring the gospel of Jesus Christ.
- Multitudes who attend church do so without any real warmth in their hearts toward the truths of God. In so doing, they make themselves like the Pharisees who drew near to God with their lips while their hearts were far from Him.

The list could go on and on.

God is so patient and kind that He does not send calamity upon us as soon as we begin breaking His laws. He gives us ample opportunities to repent and turn back to Him. But there is a limit to His patience, and when the end comes, His judgment will most certainly fall. When it does, the blame should not be placed on the God who told us how to live and who patiently put up with our sins. It should rather be placed on us for stubbornly refusing to live as God commanded and for spurning His repeated calls to us to repent.

What is repentance? Although it does not use the word, Psalm 119:59 gives us a wonderful definition:

I thought about my ways
And turned my feet to Your testimonies.

The psalmist speaks of turning his feet toward God's testimonies. We all know that it is impossible to turn toward something without simultaneously turning away from something. To turn toward God, then, is to turn away from the thing that is opposed to God. What is that thing? It is sin. To repent is to turn away from sin and to turn toward God. It is to do an about face.

We can picture it in this way. Before we repent, our faces are toward our sin and our backs toward God. In repenting, we turn our backs toward our sins and our faces toward God.

Repentance is to think so deeply and seriously about our sins that we change our behavior. And there is absolutely no point in claiming that we have repented if we have not turned our backs on our sins. The amazing thing is that when we turn our backs on our sins, God puts our sins behind His back (Isa. 38:17). The Bible also tells us that true repentance means:
- God buries our sins in the depths of the sea (Micah 7:19)
- God sweeps away our sins (Isa. 44:22)
- God removes our sins as far as the east is from the west (Ps. 103:12)
- God forgives our sins and remembers them no more (Jer. 31:34)

The hope for our nation lies in recovering true Christianity, and the hope for recovering true Christianity lies largely in Christians repenting of their sins and beginning to live again as they should have been living all along.

Savoring

From God's Word, the Bible...

Live joyfully with the wife whom you love all the days of your vain life which He has given you under the sun, all your days of vanity; for that is your portion in life, and in the labor which you perform under the sun. Whatever your hand finds to do, do it with your might; for there is no work or device or knowledge or wisdom in the grave where you are going.

Rejoice, O young man, in your youth,
And let your heart cheer you in the days of your youth;
Walk in the ways of your heart, And in the sight of your eyes;
But know that for all these
God will bring you into judgment.
Therefore remove sorrow from your heart,
And put away evil from your flesh,
For childhood and youth are vanity.

Ecclesiastes 9:9-10; 11:9-10

Adam and Eve were the first to eat of the tree of knowledge of good and evil. All of us have been eating of it ever since.

Life in this world is a mixture of good and evil. Much of our time is consumed with the evil side. We constantly hear about it: terrorism, war, conflict, political corruption, family fragmentation, hunger, child abuse, abortion, and pornography. The list goes on and on. The news reports are essentially the evil reports.

We all have to wage our personal battles with evil. We are constantly prone to lie, cheat, lust, steal, and hate. We also have a firm antipathy to doing the things that God commands us to do. We often find ourselves clenched in a vise with two jaws: the one is commission of the wrong; the other is omission of the good.

But that is only part of the story. We know evil in other ways. We get sick. Family members get sick and die. We struggle to get along with others. And finally we die. Life is a journey, and death is its end.

Because we eat so much evil from life's tree, it is entirely possible for us to become so absorbed with it that we fail to appreciate the good. As fallen creatures, we do not savor the good of life to the degree that we should.

I have often remarked that the thing that has surprised me most about life is how fast it goes. It passes with blinding speed. It is very easy to come to its end with searing regret. We may very well regret the evil we have done and the good we have failed to do. A good part of our regret may be the good we failed to savor.

For a lot of people, life is something that happens while they are busy with other things. I don't want life just to happen. I want to savor it, and I want to help others savor it as well.

By the way, to savor something is to give ourselves to the enjoyment of it. How many of life's truly significant moments pass without our realizing their significance! When Sylvia and I had little boys, a part of each day was spent picking them up and carrying them. There were times when it was inconvenient. But our little boys grew, and one day, without realizing it, I put each one down, never to pick him up again. I have often thought that if I had known that I was holding my sons in my arms for the last time, I would have held them a lot longer. I would have savored the moment.

In calling you to savor the good things of this world, I am not suggesting that you live as if this world is all that there is. Quite the opposite! Nothing so enhances our enjoyment of this world as the confidence that we are prepared for the next. By the way, that world, free as it will be from all sin and sorrow, will be the place where we will truly and fully savor our new life. And the only way to enter that world is through faith in Christ. Here is a touch of irony for you—it is only as we look beyond this world to that better world that we are truly able to enjoy our *present* world.

So I call you to savor the good things of this world as well as those things that prepare us for the next—savor God, the glorious gospel of Christ, the Bible, the preaching of the Bible, the church, the beauties of creation, the privilege of worship, marriage, and children. Let us always seek to remember these words from Stephen Vincent Benet: "Life is not lost by dying. It is lost moment by moment in a thousand uncaring ways."

Then there are these words from Thomas S. Monson: "The past is behind; learn from it. The future is ahead; prepare for it. The present is here; live it."

"Trusting in My Father's Wise Bestowment..."

From God's Word, the Bible...

For I know the thoughts that I think toward you, says the Lord, thoughts of peace and not of evil, to give you a future and a hope.

Jeremiah 29:11

Day by day, and with each passing moment,
Strength I find to meet my trials here;
Trusting in my Father's wise bestowment,
I've no cause for worry or for fear.
He, whose heart is kind beyond all measure,
Gives unto each day what He deems best,
Lovingly its part of pain and pleasure,
Mingling toil with peace and rest.

(Day by Day, Lina Sandell)

Lina Sandell knew about trials, having seen her father, a Lutheran pastor, fall from the boat in which they were sailing and drown. We might be inclined to think that such a heartbreaking event would have caused this young woman (she was twenty-six at the time) to renounce her faith in God. Harsh questions must have besieged her. Could God not have prevented this tragedy? If so, why would He allow it to happen? And why would He allow it to happen to a family who loved and served Him?

Amazingly, Lina Sandell found comfort in God. Specifically, she found comfort in His "wise bestowment." How much is packed in those two words! With the word "bestowment," Lina was registering her conviction that the Christian's trials do not come because of lapses or breakdowns in God's governance of the universe. There are no cracks in heaven for things to slip through! Our trials come to us because our Father in heaven bestows them upon us. He gives them to us.

Why would God make such bestowments? That's where the word "wise" must come in. God governs our circumstances with infinite wisdom. We are not going to understand God's working in our lives if we insist on believing that God's major concern is to bring us as much comfort and ease as possible. But what if God's concern is to conform us to the image of His Son (Rom. 8:29)? What if God is seeking our spiritual maturity instead of our temporal happiness? Does it not make sense to say that God will govern our lives one way if He is seeking our ease and a totally different way if He is seeking our maturity?

Lina Sandell was undoubtedly familiar with the Old Testament account of Joseph. What bestowments Joseph experienced! Hated by his brothers! Sold into slavery! Falsely accused and wrongly imprisoned! But through these wise bestowments, God was wisely at work to further His plan. (You can read about this in Genesis 50:20.)

"But I don't see how this circumstance could possibly further God's plan," is the common response of many people when it comes to their trials. That's where the trusting must take place. The Bible doesn't tell us that we will always understand what God is doing in a particular situation. It does tell us that God is working all things together for our good (Rom. 8:28).

Is God's heart really "kind beyond all measure"? How can we tell? Most of us tend to look at our circumstances. If they are good, we conclude that God is kind. If they are not good, we can find ourselves wondering if He is.

There is only one place to look to determine how God feels about His people, and that is the cross of Christ. God the Father put His Son on that cross—and the Son gladly and willingly went there—to rescue His people from eternal death and to give them eternal life.

That is the greatest thing God could ever do for us, and He has done it. That decisively proves His kindness. If He has done this great thing for us, are we going to allow ourselves when our circumstances turn sour to conclude that God has withdrawn His kindness? If God in kindness paid such a dear price for our salvation, are we going to entertain for a moment the notion that He is no longer kind? Why would He make the supreme expression of kindness to deal with our biggest problem—sin—only to withhold kindness in all the lesser problems that come our way? The Apostle Paul uses this logic in Romans 8:32: "He who did not spare His own Son, but delivered Him up for us all, how shall He not with Him also freely give us all things?"

All Christians want to have a strong faith. We know our faith is getting strong when we are able to believe that those very circumstances that seem to indicate that God is not kind are, in fact, proofs that He is.

Turtles All the Way Down

From God's Word, the Bible...

Moreover, brethren, I declare to you the gospel which I preached to you, which also you received and in which you stand, by which also you are saved, if you hold fast that word which I preached to you—unless you believed in vain. For I delivered to you first of all that which I also received: that Christ died for our sins according to the Scriptures, and that He was buried, and that He rose again the third day according to the Scriptures, and that He was seen by Cephas, then by the twelve. After that He was seen by over five hundred brethren at once, of whom the greater part remain to the present, but some have fallen asleep. After that He was seen by James, then by all the apostles. Then last of all He was seen by me also, as by one born out of due time.

1 Corinthians 15:1-8

A teacher asked her class why the earth doesn't fall. One boy answered: "Because it is sitting on the back of a turtle."

"And what keeps that turtle from falling?" asked the teacher.

The boy said: "Because it is sitting on the back of another turtle."

That, of course, led the teacher to ask: "And what keeps that turtle from falling?"

Deciding to put the back-and-forth conversation to an end, the boy responded: "It's turtles all the way down."

How this boy determined that the earth sits atop a huge stack of turtles is unknown!

Christians believe in the resurrection of Jesus. It is the centerpiece of their faith. Multitudes in these skeptical days put the belief of Christians in the resurrection in the same category as the boy and his turtles. As far as they are concerned, the two are one and the same. The resurrection and the turtles belong in the fantasy category! The boy invented his turtles, and Christians have invented the resurrection!

Skeptics are ever eager to put the resurrection into the turtle category because they know where it would lead if it were in the "it really happened" category—that would lead them where they do not want to go! It would cause them to admit that Jesus was God in human flesh, that what He says is true, and that He is worthy of our worship and devotion. So they deny, deny, deny.

The Apostle Paul had the resurrection of Jesus firmly in the turtle category for a considerable time. Regarding Christians as both deluded and dangerous, he decided to make it his life's work to rid his world of them. But on his way to Damascus he was hit with evidence that he could not ignore. The resurrected, living Christ appeared to him and moved his thinking from the turtle category to the reality category (Acts 9).

The little boy evidently believed in the stack of turtles because that is what he wanted to believe. He had no evidence for it, but Christians do not believe in the resurrection of Jesus merely because they want to. No, the risen Christ has not appeared to each and every Christian as He did to Paul, but there is still plenty of evidence. The heavy stone sealing the tomb was rolled away, angels were present, the Roman guards were in something of a stupor, the tomb was empty, and the linen strips in which the body of Jesus was wrapped were in a convincing configuration (Matt. 28, Mark 16, Luke 24, John 20). And the risen Christ began appearing to His disciples. He even appeared to five hundred people on one occasion (1 Cor. 15:6).

All of these evidences led the Lord Chief Justice of England, Lord Darlington, to observe: "No intelligent jury in the world could fail to bring in a verdict that the resurrection story is true."

Dr. Paul L. Maier, professor of ancient history at Western Michigan University, adds: "If all the evidence is weighed carefully and fairly, it is indeed justifiable according to the canons of historical research, to conclude that the tomb in which Jesus was buried was actually empty on the morning of the first Easter. . . . No shred of evidence has been discovered which would disprove this statement."

Christians merely ask skeptics to admit that there is convincing evidence for Jesus' resurrection and not to put us in the turtle category for going where that evidence leads. We further ask skeptics to admit that their refusal to believe in the resurrection does not have to do with lack of evidence but with an unwillingness to go where that evidence leads. Harvard law professor, Simon Greenleaf, says: "All that Christianity asks of men. . . is, that they would be consistent with themselves; that they would treat its evidences as they treat the evidence of other things. . ."

Do you believe in the truth of the resurrection of Jesus? You may have full confidence in the Bible's account!

January 29

True Riches

From God's Word, the Bible…

But He said to him, "Man, who made Me a judge or an arbitrator over you?" And He said to them, "Take heed and beware of covetousness, for one's life does not consist in the abundance of the things he possesses." Then He spoke a parable to them, saying: "The ground of a certain rich man yielded plentifully. And he thought within himself, saying, 'What shall I do, since I have no room to store my crops?' So he said, 'I will do this: I will pull down my barns and build greater, and there I will store all my crops and my goods. And I will say to my soul, "Soul, you have many goods laid up for many years; take your ease; eat, drink, and be merry."' But God said to him, 'Fool! This night your soul will be required of you; then whose will those things be which you have provided?' So is he who lays up treasure for himself, and is not rich toward God."

Luke 12:14-21

Jesus tells a story about a farmer who raises such a bumper crop that he has no place to store it. He decides to solve the problem by replacing his old barns with greater ones.

There is nothing wrong with this man taking thought to the matter of storing his crop or with him planning to build larger barns. The wrong comes in what he goes on to say: "And I will say to my soul, 'Soul, you have many goods laid up for many years; take your ease; eat, drink, and be merry.'"

Here is a statement of glaring omissions. No thought is given to the uncertain nature of earthly riches. We can have them one day, and they can be gone the next! This man acts as if he can count on them.

No thought is given to the certainty of death. He acts as if he will be on this earth forever. He does not hear the steady footfall of approaching death.

Nothing is said to indicate that he regards his wealth as a stewardship with which to honor God and bring blessing to others. No thought is given to God as the Giver of the bounty he enjoys and as the One before whom he must finally stand and give account.

It is obvious that this man is counting on his crop, his barns, and a long string of days with which to enjoy them. The thing he is not counting on is what happens. He hears the voice of God: "You fool! This night your soul will be required of you; then whose will those things be which you have provided?"

Now his crops and his barns are all worthless. They have no power to help him. They cannot stave off death, and they cannot prepare him for the eternity into which he must go. Now he wishes he had thought less about preparing for his ease and more about preparing his soul.

Jesus' story, then, is about the folly of allowing ourselves to be so consumed with the things of this world that we fail to be rich toward God.

What does it mean to be rich toward God? It means to be rich in knowledge, knowing God is our Creator and will finally be our Judge, and knowing that He is a holy God and demands that we be holy as well. It is being rich in the knowledge of ourselves, realizing that we do not possess the righteousness God demands but are, in fact, sinners. It is being rich in the knowledge of the grace of God, knowing that He, the holy God, is also the God of infinite grace. It is being rich in the knowledge of Christ, realizing that the God of grace sent the Lord Jesus to this world to do all for sinners what we could not do for ourselves. It is knowing that Jesus lived the perfect life that God demands and received in His death on the cross the penalty that we deserve for our sins. It is being rich in faith, understanding that we cannot add anything to what Christ has done for sinners but can only receive it as a gift. It is being rich in humility, knowing that we are unworthy and undeserving of God's favor. It is being rich in righteousness, receiving through faith the righteousness of Christ that qualifies us to stand acceptably in the presence of God. It is to be rich in forgiveness, rejoicing in the fact that our sins are fully and completely forgiven by God through Christ. It is being rich in hope, which means those who have been forgiven eagerly look forward to that day in which they will be received into the glories of heaven.

Rich in grace! Rich in glory! Those are the true riches, and they belong to all who will receive the Lord Jesus Christ as their Lord and Savior.

Things I Miss

From God's Word, the Bible...

These things I write to you, though I hope to come to you shortly; but if I am delayed, I write so that you may know how you ought to conduct yourself in the house of God, which is the church of the living God, the pillar and ground of the truth. And without controversy great is the mystery of godliness:
God was manifested in the flesh,
Justified in the Spirit,
Seen by angels,
Preached among the Gentiles,
Believed on in the world,
Received up in glory.

1 Timothy 3:14-16

Since my retirement from the pastorate, my wife and I have had the opportunity to attend services in several churches. We have seen preachers in blue jeans and heard lots of strumming on guitars. In one service we saw a pastor leap on a table to demonstrate the meaning of faith. He told us that he would not have made the leap if he had not had faith in the table.

Then there was the youth pastor who demonstrated the power of God for us by bundling together a few sheets of paper and ripping apart the bundle.

One of the churches in our city made headlines in the newspaper by setting the world record for the time it took to fasten a man to a wall with duct tape. My wife and I read the article and were glad that we were not there!

Still further, we have read about preachers using various props to make their sermons more "authentic." One pastor offered a series of sermons on marital relations with a bed on the platform. Another preached a sermon from a motorboat to show his congregation that they must be willing to "get out of the boat" and engage in heroic exploits for God.

Our experiences in churches and what we have read about churches have served me well. They have made me acutely aware of things I miss.

I miss the sense of eternity. It is very easy to attend service after service these days and hear little or nothing about anything beyond this life. One could easily get the impression that this life lasts forever. Meanwhile the Bible constantly affirms that this life speeds by and will soon be over. What then?

I miss the gospel, which is the good news of what God has done in and through His Son, Jesus Christ, to prepare sinners for eternity. It is the good news of Christ taking our humanity, living without sin, dying a special kind of death (in which He received the wrath of God in the place of His people), and rising from the grave and ascending to the right hand of God. One could never guess from most sermons that Christianity was designed by God to rescue law-breaking, God-hating, judgment-facing sinners through the saving work of Jesus Christ. It is, rather, very easy to draw the conclusion that Christianity is something that merely helps people cope with the stresses, strains, and challenges of daily living.

I miss seriousness. I am weary of the seemingly boundless urge to create a sense of frivolity and hilarity in services. One would never know from observing many pastors these days that they are, according to the Apostle Paul, to be "grave" or "sober-minded" (1 Tim. 3:2)—that is, serious about serious things.

I miss prayer, real prayer, that is. Most public praying I hear is so shallow, light, and breezy that no one could possibly conclude that prayer can and should lay hold of God.

I miss the loud, robust singing of the great hymns of the church that call us away from our self-centeredness and urge us to ponder God and be "lost in wonder, love and praise."

I miss the spirit of expectancy. I remember times in which God's people so looked forward to being in the house of God that they could hardly wait for services to begin.

I miss powerful, Spirit-anointed preaching. While I applaud the emphasis in recent years on expository preaching, I must say preaching is more than accurately explaining a passage of Scripture. It is possible to be straight as a gun barrel theologically, and just as empty.

I miss the reverence that is inevitably produced by the awareness that we are in the presence of God—and His is always a holy presence.

And I miss services in which the focus is on God alone instead of the constant parade of services that "recognize" policemen, firemen, community leaders, military veterans, current military personnel, and sports teams that have won championships.

I am constantly baffled by pastors and churches that feel it is necessary to have services that "honor America" even while this country plunges deeper and deeper into godlessness.

I'm sure many will respond to these things by saying: "Times are different." Yes, they are. But are they better?

In all the things I miss, I am nevertheless thankful that the Lord Jesus Christ is Head of the church and that, in the final state of glory, He, the Sovereign King, will receive all the honor and all the glory.

Astonishing Love

From God's Word, the Bible...

Behold what manner of love the Father has bestowed on us, that we should be called children of God! Therefore the world does not know us, because it did not know Him. Beloved, now we are children of God; and it has not yet been revealed what we shall be, but we know that when He is revealed, we shall be like Him, for we shall see Him as He is. And everyone who has this hope in Him purifies himself, just as He is pure.

1 John 3:1-3

The Apostle John begins this passage with an exclamation. It is an exclamation of astonishment.

John had seen more astonishing things than any man his age: Jesus healing the sick, casting out demons, stilling storms, feeding multitudes and even raising the dead. John was present on the mount when Jesus temporarily pulled back his robe of humanity so his heavenly glory could be seen. To top it all, John had also seen the risen Christ.

It would seem that John had seen so much that nothing could now astonish him. Not so! As an old man he still feels astonishment and expresses it here. And the thing that astonishes him is God's love. John calls us away from dull familiarity with that love.

John Cotton says: "The Apostle doth here correct our squint." Christians have a tendency to squint at the love of God. Let's carefully read John's words so we can completely open our eyes to see anew God's astonishing love.

What is it about that love that is so thrilling? John answers by pointing to two things.

What the love of God has already done

The love of God has bestowed on believers the title "children of God." John could lay claim to many titles: apostle, author of Scripture, pastor, but this one most thrilled him—child of God! And this is what he wanted his readers to be thrilled about—that they also could lay claim to the title "children of God."

But it was more than a title. It was a reality. So John, according to some translations, writes: "And so we are."

We will never appreciate this privilege as we should until we understand the incredibly wide chasm represented by two words in this text: "Father" and "us."

The Father is light without any hint of darkness at all (1:5). This means

God is perfectly holy. And us? We are anything but holy! God has given us commands to obey, and we have broken every one, again and again.

This chasm is infinitely wide! We could not cross it, and God did not have to do anything to cross it! But here is His love—He did cross it in and through His Son, the Lord Jesus Christ. In love for sinners, God sent Jesus to live the life those sinners have refused to live, and to die the death they deserved to die.

Now on the basis on what Jesus did, God freely and gladly invites sinners everywhere to come to Christ and be saved, pardoned and forgiven.

John could not get over this love. So he exclaims: "What manner of love is this!" Literally translated, John writes: "From what country is this kind of love?" It is as if he is saying: "I am familiar with various kinds of love. I have a category for this kind and that kind, but I have no category for the love of God for sinners. It transcends all my categories."

What the love of God will yet do

That same love is going to take all of God's children into an unspeakably glorious future.

There is in verse two an intermingling of the uncertain and the certain. What is uncertain? John writes: ". . .it has not yet been revealed what we shall be. . ." (v.2). The full details about "what we shall be" have not been released yet. The future of the children of God will be of such a nature that the greatest flights of imagination of which we are now capable can get us nowhere near the total reality. What shall we be? We will have to wait and see!

But the uncertainty John expresses has to do only with the specific details. He is not expressing uncertainty about the future itself. To the contrary, he emphatically adds: ". . .but we know that when He is revealed, we shall be like Him, for we shall see Him as He is" (v.2).

God's children are not uncertain about Jesus coming again. That's in the blessed "we know" category. Furthermore, God's children are not uncertain about being like Him. That's also in the "we know" category.

Jesus is going to come for His people; they are going to see Him and be transformed into His likeness. Paul says: "For our citizenship is in heaven, from which we also eagerly wait for the Savior, the Lord Jesus Christ, who will transform our lowly body that it may be conformed to His glorious body, according to the working by which He is able even to subdue all things to Himself" (Phil. 3:20,21).

While these things are in the future, they significantly influence the present. This is the future with a present punch. So John adds: "And everyone who has this hope in Him, purifies himself, just as He is pure" (v.3). If by the grace of God we are anticipating future glory, we will make it our business to live holy lives in this present world.

THE MONTH OF FEBRUARY

The "Thumbs-Up" Man

... And 30 Other Bible-Based Meditations

He would be driving to his work in his old pickup truck and I would be driving to my study. I used to tease him about that truck. It had so many holes in it that I dubbed it a "see-through" truck. What I most remember about those meetings is not the sight of his beat-up pickup. It is rather what Pete would do when he spotted me. He would smile and give me the thumbs-up sign. I never felt like I needed an explanation. I took his thumbs-up sign to mean: "Be encouraged! Everything is going to be okay!"

This month's readings include contributios from all four members of the Ellsworth family: Roger, Sylvia, and their sons, Tim and Martyn.

The "Thumbs-Up" Man

(A Reading from Roger)

From God's Word, the Bible...

But I do not want you to be ignorant, brethren, concerning those who have fallen asleep, lest you sorrow as others who have no hope. For if we believe that Jesus died and rose again, even so God will bring with Him those who sleep in Jesus. For this we say to you by the word of the Lord, that we who are alive and remain until the coming of the Lord will by no means precede those who are asleep. For the Lord Himself will descend from heaven with a shout, with the voice of an archangel, and with the trumpet of God. And the dead in Christ will rise first. Then we who are alive and remain shall be caught up together with them in the clouds to meet the Lord in the air. And thus we shall always be with the Lord. Therefore comfort one another with these words.

1 Thessalonians 4:13-18

It was a long time ago, but it is still firmly etched in my mind. What's that? The image of meeting Lester Auten very early each weekday morning! He would be driving to his work in his old pickup truck and I would be driving to my study. I used to tease him about that truck. It had so many holes in it that I dubbed it a "see-through" truck.

The thing I most remember about those Monday-through-Friday meetings is not the sight of his beat-up pickup. It is rather what Pete—that's what we called him—would do when he spotted me. He would smile and give me the thumbs-up sign. I never asked him about it. I never felt like I needed an explanation. I took his thumbs-up sign to mean: "Be encouraged! Everything is going to be okay!"

I know God is in control and that He makes no mistakes, but in my little, limited perspective, Pete left us much too soon. He died at age fifty-six on March 1, 1996. It was a crushing loss.

Pete was a good and godly man. He was a churchman. He loved his church and was very concerned to protect her from apathy, heresy, and division. He had little patience with those who spoke ill of her or of her pastor.

Pete had no say over the date of his birth or the date of his death. But he sure had a lot to say about that dash between the two, and he said it very well.

I'm sure Pete had his critics and detractors, but I never heard anyone speak disparagingly of him. The men of his Bible class thought so highly of him that they re-named their class after his death. What did they call it? The Thumbs-Up Class!

Ask me today about Pete Auten, and I will say "Faithful friend and a joy forever."

It was the gospel of Christ that made Pete the man he was. He loved the gospel. In his younger years, he came to see the reality and the depth of his sins and that he was not in himself prepared to stand in the presence of the holy God. He also came to see that the Lord Jesus went to the cross of Calvary to receive the wrath of God in the place of sinners. Because Jesus received it, no wrath remains for all who repent of their sins and trust in Him and the work He did on that cross. Pete could joyfully sing John Newton's words:

Amazing grace! How sweet the sound,
That saved a wretch like me!
I once was lost, but now am found,
Was blind, but now I see.

'Twas grace that taught my heart to fear,
And grace my fears relieved;
How precious did that grace appear
The hour I first believed!

It fell to me to preach at Pete's funeral. I've had to do lots of hard things in my years as a pastor, but that, I think, has to rank as the hardest of them all. In the sermon, I made mention of meeting Pete each weekday and of him smiling and giving me the thumbs-up sign. In my closing words, I expressed my firm conviction that I will, because of the glorious grace of Christ, see Pete again. I fully expect when I encounter him in the air (1 Thess. 4:17) to see him flash that familiar thumbs-up sign once again. And there everything will finally be okay. I will not be there because of anything good I have done, and he will not be there because of anything good he did. We will both be there because of the good Jesus did for us by His perfect life and atoning death.

February 2

The Terrible, Terrific Moment

(A Reading from Roger)

From God's Word, the Bible...

Now we know that whatever the law says, it says to those who are under the law, that every mouth may be stopped, and all the world may become guilty before God. Therefore by the deeds of the law no flesh will be justified in His sight, for by the law is the knowledge of sin.

Romans 3:19-20

As a teenager, William R. Newell was so rebellious that he brought continual heartache to his parents. His father, a pastor, pleaded with R.A. Torrey, President of Moody Bible College, to accept his son as a student. Torrey refused. The father continued to plead, and Torrey finally agreed.

While he was at Moody, Newell encountered the Word of God in a new and powerful way and became a Christian. What did God's Word do for him? He gives us the answer in his well-known hymn *At Calvary*:

By God's Word at last my sin I learned
Then I trembled at the law I'd spurned.

It was for Newell both a terrible and terrific moment. Terrible? Absolutely! It is a terrible thing to learn the truth about ourselves. And the truth is that we are all sinners, and sin is an awesomely horrible thing. What is sin? It is refusing to conform to what God requires. It is refusing to live according to God's laws. It is thumbing our noses in the face of our Creator and saying, "We will not live they way You want us to live. We will live the way we want to live."

God is not only our Creator. He is also our Judge. We must all give account of ourselves to Him (Rom. 14:12; Heb. 9:27). If we stand before Him in our sins, He will most surely drive us from His presence.

For several years Newell had lived without regard to his sins or to the God that he was destined to meet. He had lived in "vanity and pride." But in that terrible moment when he was confronted by God's Word, he "trembled" at the law, God's law, that he had "spurned." To spurn something is to reject it with an attitude of contempt or disdain.

Imagine it! Going through life without knowing anything about God's laws or knowing about them and not caring! Then it hits you one day that this God is real, that you have to meet Him, and all your life you have been a "spurner." You go through the Ten Commandments, and you realize that you have broken each one again and again. You are a law-breaker who must stand before the law-giver. It's no wonder that Newell said he "trembled at the law" he had "spurned." How could he, a law-breaker, ever stand acceptably in the presence of the holy law-giver?

But Newell's terrible moment was also his terrific moment. When people realize that they are sinners and begin to tremble over their sins and the judgment to come, they are in a position to receive God's remedy for law-breakers. That remedy? It is Calvary, the place where the Lord Jesus Christ was crucified.

By the grace of God, Newell came to understand that Jesus was not on that cross to pay for His own law-breaking because He, Jesus, never broke any of God's laws (1 John 3:5). He was there to receive the penalty for our law-breaking—eternal separation from God—so all who received Him would never have to pay that same penalty. What an astounding thing! On the cross, the law-giver took the penalty of law-breakers! And because Jesus took it, there is now no penalty for those who do as Newell did and turn to Christ.

In his hymn, Newell looks back over his life and expresses double amazement. He is amazed at how he had lived and amazed that there could be pardon for one who had lived as he had. Try to imagine the joy he felt when he penned these lines:

Mercy there was great, and grace was free;
Pardon there was multiplied to me;
There my burdened soul found liberty,
At Calvary.

In John Bunyan's *The Pilgrim's Progress,* the major character, Christian, came to the cross, gave three leaps for joy, and went on singing. . .

Thus far did I come laden with my sin,
Nor could aught ease the grief that I was in,
Till I came hither. What a place is this!
Must here be the beginning of my bliss!

The greatest of all knowledge is to know ourselves to be sinners. It will be terrible when we come to know that, but that knowledge will lead us on to that which is terrific indeed—salvation through Christ.

Our Gulf-Spanning God

(A Reading from Sylvia)

From God's Word, the Bible...

For there is one God and one Mediator between God and men, the Man Christ Jesus, who gave Himself a ransom for all, to be testified in due time...

1 Timothy 2:5-6

The great hymns of the church are a wonderful part of our Christian heritage. They teach great biblical truths and express our praise to God for those truths. Many hymns have nuggets of gold in the space of just a few words. The hymn *At Calvary*, written by William R. Newell, has these words at the end of verse 4:

Oh, the mighty gulf that God did span
At Calvary.

Have you ever given much thought to the mighty gulf that God spanned at Calvary? The more you understand about that mighty gulf, the more precious your salvation will become to you. What is that mighty gulf? It is the vast expanse between a holy God and sinful man. It is an expanse so very wide that no man can bridge it on his own. In fact no one, no matter how good he perceives himself to be, can even come close to bridging that gap.

We know that God is holy, but it isn't easy for us to comprehend exactly what that means. God is perfect in every aspect of His being. He is perfectly perfect. We also know that we are sinners. But that, too, is difficult for us to completely comprehend. Just as every aspect of God's being is perfect, so every aspect of our being is tainted with sin. Our sinful actions, our sinful words, our sinful thoughts are ever present in our lives as sins of commission. And then there are the sins of omission—the good actions we fail to do, the kind, positive words we fail to speak, and the godly thoughts we fail to entertain.

There is indeed a mighty gulf between sinful man and holy God that we cannot possibly span. But if we are ever to be acceptable to God and to have any hope of God letting us into heaven (Rev. 21:27), that gulf must somehow be spanned. God cannot un-god himself and come down to our level, and we cannot make ourselves perfect, no matter how hard we try.

So God in His great wisdom devised a plan to span that gap. His Son, Jesus Christ, became the God-man by taking our humanity without divesting himself of His deity. He lived the perfect life required of us that we cannot possibly live. He went to Calvary's cross and became sin for us and there received the wrath of God against that sin in our place (2 Cor. 5:21). A marvelous exchange takes place for believers. Jesus took our sin and we get His righteousness. God accepted what Jesus did as evidenced by the resurrection. Thus Jesus Christ became the bridge that spanned that great gulf between sinful man and holy God.

And why did God go to such great length to do this? The hymn writer gives us the answer in the first lines of this same verse:

Oh, the love that drew salvation's plan!
Oh, the grace that brought it down to man!

It was God's great love for us and His grace to us that moved His heart to devise salvation's plan and bring it down to man. In our limited knowledge, we cannot fully comprehend that kind of love and grace. In eternity I believe that God will reveal to us layer after layer of His great love and grace, and we will forever praise Him for salvation's plan. What a God of wisdom, love, and grace we serve! Oh, the mighty gulf that God did span at Calvary. All praise and glory to our great gulf-spanning God.

Saying Goodbye to a World of Goodbyes

(A Reading from Roger)

From God's Word, the Bible...

These all died in faith, not having received the promises, but having seen them afar off were assured of them embraced them and confessed that they were strangers and pilgrims on the earth. For those who say such things declare plainly that they seek a homeland. And truly if they had called to mind that country from which they had come out, they would have had opportunity to return. But now they desire a better, that is, a heavenly country. Therefore God is not ashamed to be called their God, for He has prepared a city for them.

Hebrews 11:13-16

I have often had to say "Goodbye." Many times it has been a pleasure. When I completed my years of education, it was a joy to say goodbye to boring lectures, tons of homework, and tests. I shall never forget saying goodbye to the hospital where I had surgery to repair a skull fracture. That was a wonderful goodbye indeed.

But the majority of my goodbyes have been painful. A few years back, I had to say goodbye to my father, and a few years after that to my mother. There have been goodbyes to churches I have served as pastor. Those have always been difficult. And there have been goodbyes to dear friends.

Dog-lovers will understand this (and if you're not one, please go to the next paragraph)—it is exceedingly hard to say goodbye to a true and loyal canine friend.

I realize that I have had to say fewer goodbyes than some, and many of my goodbyes have not been as difficult as those experienced by others. I try to keep these things in mind so I can keep my balance and not turn my life into an ongoing pity party. But I have had my share, and I am sure you have as well. This is a world of goodbyes.

My sad goodbyes here make me look forward to that time in which I will be able to say a final goodbye—a goodbye to this world of goodbyes!

Yes, I am looking forward to that world in which there will be no more goodbyes. I'm talking about that world the Bible calls heaven.

Heaven consists of two stages or states. There is the intermediate state and the final state. The intermediate state is the one which the soul enters when the believer dies. His or her body goes into the grave, and the soul goes to be with God. But that is not the final state. The Lord Jesus is going to come again, bringing as He comes the souls of all believers who have died. He is going to raise the bodies of believers and those bodies, modeled after His own resurrection body, will be rejoined to those souls. In those resurrected, glorified bodies, believers will inhabit what is described in Revelation 21 and 22, that is, a new earth which will have one glorious city—the New Jerusalem (Rev. 21:2).

One feature of that new world puzzled me for a long time. The Apostle John says: " . . .there was no more sea" (Rev. 21:1). I wondered about that. Why will there be no sea on that new earth? Then it occurred to me that the sea has often been the place of separation or the place of sad goodbyes. One loved one is on the ship while another stands on the shore, and they wave goodbye. There will be no such separation in heaven and no need to say goodbye. This is the destiny of all who have repented of their sins and trusted in the Lord Jesus Christ as their Savior.

While I wait for my new body and my new world, and while I continue to say sad goodbyes here, I try to sing along with Squire Parsons:

I'm kind of homesick for a country
To which I've never been before.
No sad goodbyes will there be spoken
For time won't matter anymore.

Beulah Land, I'm longing for you
And some day on thee I'll stand.
There my home shall be eternal.
Beulah Land, sweet Beulah Land.

I'm looking now across the river
Where my faith will end in sight.
There's just a few more days to labor.
Then I will take my heavenly flight.[1]

1 "Sweet Beulah Land Lyrics." *Lyrics.com*. STANDS4 LLC, 2017. Web. 6 Jul 2017. <http://www.lyrics.com/lyric/5214769>.

Thanks for the Thoughts

(A Reading from Roger)

From God's Word, the Bible...

Many, O Lord my God, are Your wonderful works
Which You have done;
And Your thoughts toward us
Cannot be recounted to You in order;
If I would declare and speak of them,
They are more than can be numbered.

Psalm 40:5

How often does it occur to us to give thanks to God for His thoughts toward us? We often express thanks to various ones for their thoughtfulness. Do we realize as we should that no one has been more thoughtful toward us than God?

In Psalm 40 David gives thanks to God. He begins with the particular and moves to the general. He thinks about a harrowing crisis from which God had delivered him (vv. 1-2) and that causes him to think about some general things. He thanks God for His "wonderful works" which are "many," and then he mentions the thoughts of God.

It is as if David is saying something along these lines: "This wonderful deliverance that I have experienced is just one of God's many wonderful works, and all His wonderful works flow from Him thinking about me."

So let's think about the thoughts of God and let's thank Him for the thoughts.

It occurs to me that it is a staggering thing that God would think about us at all. The chasm between God and us is too huge for words. He is almighty in strength, unlimited in wisdom, and clothed in majesty and glory. We are weak, foolish, and wear the tattered garments of sin. Yet God thinks about us! No wonder David marveled:

What is man that You are mindful of him?
(Ps. 8:4)

Then it is amazing that God has as many thoughts about us as He does. It would be a wonderful thing indeed if God had only a thought or two toward us, but His thoughts about us are "more than can be numbered" (v. 3).

David says God's thoughts "cannot be recounted . . .in order." If we were to attempt to relate all the thoughts God has had toward us in the order in which He had them, we would be attempting the impossible. It would be as impossible as moving Mt. Everest with a spoon. In Psalm 139:17-18, David says:

How precious also are Your thoughts to me, O God!
If I should count them, they would be more in number than the sand. . .

It is further amazing that God would think about us the thoughts that He thinks. Someone might be inclined to say, "I'm sure God thinks about me. He thinks about making my life miserable."

The devil would have you believe that, but he is the master of lies, and that is one of his lies. Here is what God says about His thoughts toward His people: "For I know the thoughts that I think toward you, says the LORD, thoughts of peace and not of evil, to give you a future and a hope" (Jer. 29:11).

To all of that we must add this: It is astonishing that God would think about us in the greatest way possible. And what way is that? It is God thinking about the way to forgive us of our sins and to restore us to Himself. And God found the way. That way is none other than His Son, Jesus Christ.

This fortieth Psalm is Messianic. That means it looks forward to the coming of the Lord Jesus Christ. I can hear Him say to the Father the words of verses 7 and 8:

Behold, I come;
In the scroll of the Book it is written of me.
I delight to do Your will, O my God,
And Your law is within my heart.

Jesus came to this earth in our humanity just as He and the Father had agreed. He came to do the will of the Father, that is, He came to perfectly obey the laws of God, which, of course, we have not obeyed. And His obedience was not grudging but flowed from a heart that loved the law of God.

One thing the law of God demands is payment for sin. Through His life, the Lord Jesus provided the righteousness we lack, and through His death He received the penalty for our sins.

All of this is because God thought toward us the greatest thought of all! How thankful we should be for all His thoughts and for this one thought in particular!

Even My Cap Knows I've Been Saved!

(A Reading from Roger)

From God's Word, the Bible...

Therefore, if anyone is in Christ, he is a new creation; old things have passed away; behold, all things have become new.

2 Corinthians 5:17

The words came from Burliss Hill in a Baptist testimony meeting a couple of weeks after his conversion to Christ. More about that cap in a minute!

Before he was converted, Burliss was a rough, hot-tempered man. It was my father who invited him to attend revival services at a nearby Baptist church. Burliss agreed to go. When the service was over, he angrily stomped away telling my Dad not to invite him again because he wouldn't be back. Much to my Dad's surprise, he was back the next night and for several nights in succession. Each time he went away angry and swore that he would not return. But there was an invisible hand at work drawing Burliss in.

One night my parents were awakened by someone rapping on their door. They opened the door and there stood Burliss' wife, Hilda, saying: "You've got to come, Burliss is trying to find the Lord."

My parents went. My Dad prayed with Burliss, and he was, to use a phrase that was common in those days, gloriously saved.

Now about that cap! Before he was saved, Burliss was given to great outbursts of temper. In his fits of rage he would invariably throw his cap on the ground and stomp on it. But his conversion to Christ made him a new man. Burliss knew that he was new, and, in his estimation, his cap knew as well because he had not stomped on it since he was saved!

Burliss Hill would answer God's call to preach the gospel and would become my parents' pastor and my pastor. He preached the morning that I was converted, and he baptized me in the pond of a local farmer a few days later.

Burliss was a common, ordinary man who loved the Lord and faithfully preached His Word. I will always be grateful to God for him.

I'm sure most consider me to be hopelessly out of date and old-fashioned, but I believe in those things so wonderfully portrayed in the conversion of Burliss Hill. I believe that there is such a thing as conviction of sin and that it can be so powerful that it drives sinners to despair. I believe that there is salvation in Christ for even the worst of sinners. I believe that salvation changes people, that if anyone is truly saved he is, in the words of Paul, "a new creation" and that "old things have passed away" and "all things have become new" (2 Cor. 5:17).

I often wonder these days what has happened to those days. Where are those who are under a heavy conviction from the Spirit of God? An old hymn, *Brethren, We Have Met to Worship*, refers to "trembling mourners, who are struggling hard with sin." That line must sound very strange to the few people who still sing that hymn!

Where are those who are "gloriously saved"? And why is it that so many who profess faith in Christ give no evidence of a profound change and soon fall away?

And where are the pastors who preach for a deep conviction of sin and a glorious salvation? Much preaching these days seems more interested in amusing sinners than in convicting them and pointing them to Christ. In his hymn *At Calvary*, William R. Newell says:

By God's Word at last my sin I learned;
Then I trembled at the law I'd spurned,
Till my guilty soul imploring turned
To Calvary.

It is accurate and Spirit-anointed preaching of the Word of God that makes sinners learn about their sins, to tremble at the law they have spurned, and then to turn to Calvary. But what if the Word of God is not preached as it should be? Yes, what then?

These things must ultimately come, of course, from the Spirit of God, and that leads to another question: Where are those who are crying out for an unusual and powerful outpouring of God's Spirit?

If we are not now among those crying to God, let's make it our business to be among them. And let's believe that our crying will lead the Lord to say: "And I will not hide My face from them anymore; for I shall have poured out My Spirit. . ." (Ezek. 39:29).

God Leads His Dear Children

(A Reading from Sylvia)

From God's Word, the Bible...

But now, thus says the Lord, who created you, O Jacob,
And He who formed you, O Israel:
"Fear not, for I have redeemed you;
I have called you by your name;
You are Mine.
When you pass through the waters, I will be with you;
And through the rivers, they shall not overflow you.
When you walk through the fire, you shall not be burned,
Nor shall the flame scorch you."

Isaiah 43:1-2

When I recently heard a recording of the old hymn, *God Leads Us Along*, it brought back fond memories of my childhood and teen years at Steel City Baptist Church outside Benton, Ilinois. I thought of dear Hazel Bethel Wayman singing that hymn during many church services. The hymn was written by George A. Young in 1903. Young himself was no stranger to difficulty and hardship. For many years he served as a pastor of small churches in small communities, often finding it very difficult to make ends meet financially.

That brings me back to Hazel Bethel Wayman, who was just Hazel Bethel when I first became acquainted with her. She was a single mother whose husband had left her penniless with four children and one soon to be born. She and her children lived in a tiny, run-down house. They had no automobile and were very poor even by 1950s standards. Hazel Bethel's life was extremely difficult and yet this quiet, godly lady would stand in front of our small congregation and sing without accompaniment:

Some thro' the waters, some through the flood,
Some thro' the fire, but all thro' the blood.
Some thro' great sorrow, but God gives a song
In the night season and all the day long.

Even as a child I realized that God had certainly taken this dear lady through many hardships, described as water, flood, and fire by this hymn writer. But God had also taken her through the blood of Jesus Christ and given her a song in spite of her difficult life.

The second verse has these words:

Sometimes in the valley, in darkest of night,
God leads His dear children along.

I knew Hazel Bethel had gone through many valleys of darkest night. I wondered how many sleepless nights she had spent weeping and praying for God to take care of her and her children. God answered that prayer, and all five of her children grew to be responsible adults and committed Christians.

Verse three says:

Though sorrows befall us and Satan oppose,
God leads His dear children along.
Through grace we can conquer,
Defeat all our foes;
God leads His dear children along.

By God's grace Hazel Bethel was a conqueror, defeating her foes of desertion and poverty. Her victory over being deserted by her husband was defeated by her knowledge that God had not deserted her. Her victory over poverty was not due to her becoming financially wealthy, but rather by her knowledge of the riches she possessed in Christ Jesus as her Savior and sustainer.

After her children were grown, Hazel Bethel became Hazel Wayman when God gave her a Christian husband. They enjoyed several years together before God took him home.

The last verse of this hymn has these lines:

Away from the mire, and away from the clay
God leads His dear children along;
Away up in glory, eternity's day,
God leads His dear children along.

Hazel Bethel Wayman was a living testimony to the Lord's sufficiency. She prevailed by God's grace, and she is now in the presence of her Lord and Savior, Jesus Christ, far removed from the mire and clay of this world. All her sorrows and dark nights are gone forevermore. I thank God for her life and for the godly example she was to one young girl. I remember her every time I hear that great hymn, *God Leads Us Along*.

February 8

The Way of the Righteous

(A Reading from Martyn)

From God's Word, the Bible...

Blessed is the man
Who walks not in the counsel of the ungodly,
Nor stands in the path of sinners, Nor sits in the seat of the scornful;
But his delight is in the law of the Lord,
And in His law he meditates day and night.
He shall be like a tree planted by the rivers of water,
That brings forth its fruit in its season,
Whose leaf also shall not wither; And whatever he does shall prosper.
The ungodly are not so,
But are like the chaff which the wind drives away.
Therefore the ungodly shall not stand in the judgment,
Nor sinners in the congregation of the righteous.
For the Lord knows the way of the righteous,
But the way of the ungodly shall perish.

Psalm 1

One of the most basic and fundamental truths of the Bible is that there are only two groups of people in the world. There are only two roads that people can travel. There are only two destinations to arrive at (Matt. 7:13-14).

Psalm 1 sets this division of the human race before us. It contrasts the righteous man and the ungodly man, the way of the righteous and the way of the wicked. In verses 1 to 3 the focus is on the walk or conduct of the righteous man. These verses emphasize four characteristics of the righteous man's life.

One is that it is *a blessed life* (v. 1). We often hear that when the Bible uses the word "blessed" it is using it as a synonym for "happy." It is true that the words are very similar, but the word "blessed" is a richer, fuller word. It speaks of God's favor resting upon someone, and of the joy, contentment, and fulfillment that person knows as a result of God's favor. To be blessed is to know joy in God that does not depend upon circumstances. The Bible invariably joins these things together: righteousness and blessedness, holiness and happiness, walking in the fear of the Lord and experiencing true joy and contentment.

Another characteristic of the life of the righteous is that it is *a separated life*. Verse 1 describes the righteous man's life in terms of what it is not. The godly man does not walk in the counsel of the ungodly. In other words, he rejects the godless mindset of society. His life is not governed by the popular thinking or the accepted practices or the general consensus of the day. The righteous man also does not stand in the path of sinners. Standing indicates deliberate action. The man who does this is not merely coming under the influence of godless people as he goes along his way, but he is deliberately choosing the way of sinners. By contrast the righteous man does not linger in the path of sinners. Verse 1 also tells us that the righteous man does not sit in the seat of the scornful. This is a reference to the scoffer, the man who mocks God and ridicules all that is good and right and true. The way of the righteous is a separate way. The godly man separates himself from the counsel of the ungodly, the path of sinners, and the seat of the scornful.

A third mark of the righteous man's life is that it is *a Word-saturated life* (v. 2). The godly man delights in the law of the Lord. God's Word is a delight to the righteous man, and he demonstrates his delight by meditating upon it. We all think about what we love. If the Word of God is our delight, then we will spend much time reflecting upon it, pondering it, contemplating it. The truly blessed life is a life that is saturated with the Word of God.

A *fourth characteristic* of the righteous man's life is that it is *a flourishing life*. The man who saturates his life with God's Word will flourish like the tree described in verse 3. His life will be a beautiful thing. His life will be fruitful. His life will bring glory to God and be a source of blessedness to others.

Here are four questions to pose to yourself as you meditate upon Psalm 1.

- Are these verses an accurate description of your life?
- If not, why not?
- Do you want your life to be like this?
- What changes will you make?

Every child of God is, by definition, righteous. This term in the Old Testament applies to justified sinners and not to some elite class of Christians. However, God's people frequently backslide and live at a level in which they could hardly be said to be flourishing.

The good news is that if you are currently more like a shrub in the desert than like this well-watered tree in Psalm 1, there is grace with God to renew you, refresh you, and impart health to your soul. By God's grace you can become like this flourishing tree and know more of the blessedness spoken of in this Psalm.

February 9

How Will We Be Remembered?

(A Reading from Tim)

From God's Word, the Bible...

He who troubles his own house will inherit the wind,
And the fool will be servant to the wise of heart.

Proverbs 11:29

Some time ago an unusual obituary ran in a California newspaper. It was an obituary for a seventy-nine-year-old woman. It said: "Dolores had no hobbies, made no contribution to society, and rarely shared a kind word or deed in her life."

Her daughter, the writer of the obituary, also wrote: "I speak for the majority of her family when I say her presence will not be missed by many, very few tears will be shed, and there will be no lamenting over her passing."

What a way to be remembered!

A columnist from another newspaper investigated to determine if the obituary was legitimate or a hoax. Sadly, he verified its authenticity and even spoke to the daughter about what she had written. The woman explained: "I wanted to do the right thing, the honest thing. When she died, a co-worker gave me a copy of an obituary she wrote for her father as a kind of writing guide. What struck me was how my mother was none of the things I was reading. She was never there for us, she was never good, and she left no legacy."

It calls to mind what the Bible says when the vile, idolatrous king of Judah, Jehoram, died: "He reigned in Jerusalem eight years and, to no one's sorrow, departed" (2 Chron. 21:20).

What a contrast we have in the death of the godly priest Jehoiada: "But Jehoiada grew old and was full of days, and he died; he was one hundred and thirty years old when he died. And they buried him in the City of David among the kings, because he had done good in Israel, both toward God and His house" (2 Chron. 24:15-16).

The other day I picked up a copy of the book *A Nickel's Worth of Skim Milk*, written by Bob Hastings, a Baptist minister and editor for several years of *The Illinois Baptist*. The book is his story of growing up in southern Illinois.

My childhood experiences differ considerably from his. He was a child of the Great Depression; I of the 1980s. But there's something warm about reading the stories of others as they were growing up—especially if they share fond memories.

Some of Hastings' stories made me smile. He recalled how at Christmas every year, his father would kill one of their chickens. His mom would dress it, dry it, and package it. His dad then took the chicken to the post office and mailed it to their daughter in St. Louis.

"We sent what we could, and I always sensed that the package was tied by cords of love," Hastings wrote.

Reading Hastings' childhood stories made me appreciate the fact that over the next few years, I'll be largely responsible for making memories for my own children. Those memories will accompany them throughout their lives.

Will the thoughts they have fifty years from now make them smile? I'm fairly confident that their memories will never be as bitter as the woman who wrote her mother's obituary. But am I doing all I can to brighten their days and fill their lives with joy?

Too often I find myself tempted to shortchange my children to pursue my own selfish interests. Rather than playing with my children, it's easier for me to plop down and watch a ballgame or waste time on the computer.

The sad obituary carries a potent message for parents. What will our children say about us when we're gone?

I hope my children will never be tempted to say about me what this woman said about her mother: "There will be no service, no prayers, and no closure for the family she spent a lifetime tearing apart. We cannot come together in the end to see to it that her grandchildren and great-grandchildren can say their goodbyes. So I say here for all of us, GOOD BYE MOM."

February 10

The Fretful Clock

(A Reading from Roger)

From God's Word, the Bible...

Be anxious for nothing, but in everything by prayer and supplication, with thanksgiving, let your requests be made known to God; and the peace of God, which surpasses all understanding, will guard your hearts and minds through Christ Jesus.

Philippians 4:6-7

A woman was having trouble with her old clock. It seems that the clock had become anxious and upset. So the woman took the clock to a clock counselor.

"Old clock," said the counselor, "what is bothering you?"

And the clock responded: "I've been thinking about all the ticking I have to do! That's 2 ticks per second, 120 ticks per minute, 7,200 ticks per hour, 172,800 ticks per day, 1,209,600 ticks per week and 62,899,200 ticks per year. And the more I think, the more upset I become. What if I can't get all that ticking done?"

The counselor wisely asked: "How many ticks do you have to tick at a time?"

And the clock said: "Just one tick at a time."

So the counselor said: "Then tick one tick at a time. Don't even think about the next tick, till you get this tick ticked."

With that advice in hand, the woman took the old clock home and set it on the mantel. And it has been calmly ticking along ever since.

It seems to be a silly story. Clocks don't get anxious. They don't worry about all their ticking, and they don't go to see counselors. But we do. And this imaginative bit about the clock is designed to get us to see ourselves. We are the silly ones, filled with anxious days and hurried ways, throwing away the delights of today in our dithering about tomorrow. It is a bad, mad bargain. We can't tick today because we know we will have to tick tomorrow. Far too many can say:

I worry about tomorrow, I fret over the past.
Meanwhile, today is leaving me fast.

Are we to think about tomorrow and make wise preparations for it? Yes, of course. But that is different from being anxious and worried about it.

Jesus sees us—just as He so perfectly saw the members of His audience on the day that He delivered the Sermon on the Mount. An anxious lot they were, fretting over the future. Would they be able to find clothes to wear and food to eat? They were feeling the tyranny of tomorrow.

Jesus called their attention to the birds. Small, helpless creatures in a world of dangers, they would seem to be anxious. But they are content and happy.

Jesus also pointed them to the lilies, that is, to the wildflowers that were growing in the fields without any cultivation. He essentially said to His disciples (and to others): "Become disciples of those flowers. Learn from them."

The lesson they were to draw from those flowers was this: By using the means God had established for them, the lilies are adequately sustained for the time that God has appointed for them.

If God adequately sustains the lilies for the time He has appointed for them, we may be sure that He will sustain His people for the time He has appointed for them. How can we be sure? Because God's people are far more important to Him than flowers! And how do we know that? Let the Apostle Paul answer: "He who did not spare His own Son, but delivered Him up for us all, how shall He not with Him also freely give us all things?" (Rom. 8:32).

The cross of Christ, not our circumstances, is ever the key to understanding how God feels about His people.

So the cure for fretful living is to trust God to do what is best for us. Does this mean we will never experience anything that is unpleasant? Not at all! What is best for us is to be weaned away from this world so we will seek first God's kingdom and righteousness (Matt. 6:33). That requires the Lord to take an entirely different approach with us than He would if He were concerned only about our comfort and convenience.

The key to living in this world is to not live for this world but rather to live for a higher and better world. We are called to check our priorities each day to make sure we are living for that world and then to actually live for it—one tick at a time.

Unsung Heroes

(A Reading from Sylvia)

From God's Word, the Bible...

Take heed that you do not do your charitable deeds before men, to be seen by them. Otherwise you have no reward from your Father in heaven. Therefore, when you do a charitable deed, do not sound a trumpet before you as the hypocrites do in the synagogues and in the streets, that they may have glory from men. Assuredly, I say to you, they have their reward. But when you do a charitable deed, do not let your left hand know what your right hand is doing, that your charitable deed may be in secret; and your Father who sees in secret will Himself reward you openly.

Matthew 6:1-4

He who is faithful in what is least is faithful also in much; and he who is unjust in what is least is unjust also in much.

Luke 16:10

A local television station has a weekly feature called *Unsung Heroes* which highlights individuals who are doing something to benefit others in their sphere of influence. These individuals are not seeking recognition or praise for their deeds. They simply have a servant heart that desires to help others.

The kingdom of God also has many unsung heroes. They are followers of Christ who serve God faithfully in small churches and villages around the world. They are hidden from the world's eyes, but not from God's eyes.

In his book, *To the Golden Shore*, Courtney Anderson details an account of young Adoniram Judson's struggle as to what direction his life would take. He had a desire and drive to achieve greatness and fame, perhaps as the pastor of a great church in a large city where he would have praise and thousands would come to hear him preach.

> Without realizing how it happened, he found himself comparing this minister with an obscure country pastor, humbly striving only to bring his congregation and himself to God, without any thought of self. The minister in whose place he had imagined himself was really no better than any other ambitious man, anxious only for fame.
>
> What would the judgment be on him in the next world? If he achieved heaven, he would certainly not achieve fame in heaven. It

would be the obscure country pastor whose fame would ring out there through eternity, even though he were never heard of here.[2]

When I read these words, I immediately thought of our son who has for years been pastor of a small, rural church. He labors diligently in the Word and doctrine (1 Tim. 5:17) to instruct and feed his small flock. And he is only one of many such pastors who serve faithfully in obscurity.

There are also vast numbers of unknown laymen who serve Christ their whole lives in their obscure little churches. They faithfully attend the worship services, give their tithe, pray, and minister in Christ's name to needs they see around them. They never achieve the world's fame, but they bring glory to God and advance His kingdom.

I thought of James and Katheryn Williams in the little country church where I grew up. They lived across the road from the church and were always present at every service. James did not become a Christian until he was a young adult, and although he was limited in education and shy by nature, he still found ways to serve the Lord. God had given him a powerful singing voice--and sing he did even though he could not read a note of music. For over forty years he led the congregation in singing the great hymns of the faith.

Katheryn led a girls' mission group, taught Sunday School, served as church clerk, taught in Vacation Bible School, and helped wherever else there was a need. Together James and Katheryn served as church custodians seeing to it that God's house was clean and in good condition. They are both now in the presence of the God they served so faithfully and obscurely in that little country church. But their legacy continues as their daughter, Peggy, has followed in their footsteps. Among other areas of service, Peggy has served faithfully as pianist in that same church for forty years—and counting.

God's view of heroes is far different from the world's. The world's heroes are often entertainers, athletes, and people in the public eye. God's heroes are those who have been faithful to serve Him where He has placed them, however obscure of a place that may be, and with the abilities He has given them, however limited those abilities may be. "Moreover it is required in stewards that one be found faithful" (1 Cor. 4:2). Those who have served God in obscurity will one day be rewarded openly (Matt. 6:4).

One of the joys of heaven will be to meet and learn about all the unsung heroes, the saints of God who faithfully served the Master in unknown places. Great will be their reward in heaven.

2 *To the Golden Shore: The Life of Adoniram Judson*, Judson Press, Valley Forge, 1987, p.29

Wisdom for the Life Business

(A Reading from Roger)

From God's Word, the Bible...

"Now therefore, listen to me, my children,
For blessed are those who keep my ways.
Hear instruction and be wise,
And do not disdain it.
Blessed is the man who listens to me,
Watching daily at my gates,
Waiting at the posts of my doors.
For whoever finds me finds life,
And obtains favor from the Lord;
But he who sins against me wrongs his own soul;
All those who hate me love death."

Proverbs 8:32-36

We are all in the "life" business, and this is challenging business indeed. The bad news about this business is that it is very easy to mess it up. Many make life harder than it needs to be. They make poor choices, and poor choices lead to painful consequences. Poor choices sometimes bring life to an early end. In other cases, they can cause us to live with pain and heartache for years and years.

The Book of Proverbs is about the life business. It tells us what we can do to make life less challenging and more rewarding. Its message in one word? Wisdom! We have to be wise to master the life business. What is wisdom? It is knowing how to live. It is seeing and doing the right thing in the situations that life presents. It is essentially insight. It is making the right choices in life, choices that enable us to reap the good that life has to offer us.

If we live wisely, we will reap the good life has to offer. A little boy, trying to pick out a puppy, saw one wagging his tail, and said: "I want the one with the happy ending."

Making wise choices in life enables us to be happy at the end of the situation for which we are choosing. It should be obvious, then, that nothing is more important than getting wisdom (Prov. 4:7).

In Proverbs 8:32-36, the author steps aside, as it were, and allows wisdom herself to speak directly to us. And what does she have to say? The first thing is a command. She commands us to listen to her (v. 32).

She is offering us her services, but her offer will not help us if we refuse to listen! It's interesting that she refers to us as her "children." We should not take this as a compliment! Children are notorious for not listening! Children are, of course, very limited in knowledge. They rush ahead without thinking. They are easily deceived. They often refuse to exert the diligence that is necessary to learn. They prefer entertainment and excitement to learning. All of these traits are found in many adults when it comes to the matter of wisdom for living.

As wisdom continues to speak, she tells us what is necessary for listening—effort!

She pictures herself as living in a house. Each day she comes out of her front door and speaks to those who are waiting outside. Those who make the effort to be at her house reap the benefit of hearing her. They get insights on how to live. And it requires effort on their part! In order to be at wisdom's gates, one has to get up out of his bed, get dressed, make the journey to wisdom's house, and wait for her to appear.

How should we relate this to ourselves? The voice of wisdom speaks to us in the Bible. What must we do to hear her voice? We must read the Bible, hear it preached and taught, read good books about it, discuss it with others, and try to memorize key verses. Sadly enough, many people want the life skills that the Bible offers without having to put forth the effort to get them!

Finally, wisdom tells us the result of listening and the result of refusing to listen. The result of listening is blessing, which is a favor or benefit from God (vv. 32, 35). The result of not listening is calamity (v. 36).

There are temporal blessings for those who heed the voice of wisdom: longer life (3:2; 9:11; 10:2), peace of mind (3:2), favor with God and man (3:4; 12:2), direction (3:6), physical well-being (3:8), material well-being (3:10), happiness (3:13), stability (12:3).

But the greatest of all the blessings offered by wisdom is spiritual life here and now, and eternal life in the future. The Bible constantly sets the way of life and the way of death before us. The voice of wisdom urges us to choose life by trusting in the Lord Jesus Christ and His redeeming work.

Those who reject the voice of wisdom in the gospel "wrong" their souls and "love death" (v. 36).

Words to the Bride

(A Reading from Martyn)

From God's Word, the Bible...

Listen, O daughter,
Consider and incline your ear;
Forget your own people also, and your father's house;
So the King will greatly desire your beauty;
Because He is your Lord, worship Him.
And the daughter of Tyre will come with a gift;
The rich among the people will seek your favor.

Psalm 45:10-12
(Read the whole of Psalm 45 for this meditation.)

Psalm 45 is a celebration of a royal wedding. Like many of the Psalms it looks beyond the immediate circumstances that accompanied its writing and anticipates the glories of Jesus Christ.

The Bible frequently uses the imagery of a bridegroom and a bride to picture the relationship between Christ and His church. We are on solid ground in interpreting this Psalm as an anticipation of the wedding between Christ and His bride, the church. There are some words spoken to the bride in verses 10 to 12. They are words of exhortation and reassurance.

The first word of exhortation is "Forget" (v. 10). The bride is told to forget her own people and her father's house. It is not that she is to forget her family and her people in an absolute sense. The idea is that she is to be so thrilled by her husband that she does not long for her old life. The same exhortation is to be given to Jesus' bride, the church. We are to forget our old life. We are to leave it behind and cling to our Beloved (see Matt. 10:37 and Luke 14:26). Having been united to Christ, we are not to pine after the world and long for its company and its pleasures.

The second word of exhortation is "Worship" (v. 11). The bride of Christ is to honor and worship her Lord. Jesus is the sovereign Lord over all things, and all people owe Him worship. For His bride, it is a delight to obey this exhortation. As a wife finds it a delight to honor the husband whom she highly respects, so the church delights to worship her Husband, whose glories are described in the first nine verses of this psalm.

These verses also contain two words of assurance. Brides may at times have doubts. They may be in need of reassurance. So it is with the church. We sometimes struggle with doubts. Thankfully, there is much in God's Word to reassure us.

The first word of assurance is "The King desires you" (v. 11). One of the doubts that might trouble a bride is that her husband may not be pleased with her. The bride in this psalm is told there is no cause for such doubts. She is assured that the King will "greatly desire" her beauty. God's people know something about these doubts. Jesus' bride can think of endless reasons to be enthralled by His beauty but not a single reason why He should desire her. But God's Word assures us that Jesus greatly desires His bride. He takes pleasure in her not because she is beautiful in and of herself. Her beauty is all from Him. He has beautified her as an act of His grace and for His glory.

What a blessed thing it is to read in God's Word the reassuring words of Jesus' love for His own! The Bible tells us Jesus loves His bride and died for her. His thoughts for her cannot be numbered. He will return for her and draw her to His side. Nothing will ever separate her from His love. What blessed assurances these are!

The second word of assurance is "The nations will honor you" (v. 12). The idea in this verse is that people of high rank and great wealth from other nations will honor the King and His bride. Because of her closeness to the King, the bride will be honored and her favor will be sought.

Today, wherever the gospel triumphs among the nations, the bride of Christ is loved and honored. Wherever the King is worshiped, His queen is held in high regard. In this life, the people of God are hated, despised, and persecuted. But God's Word assures us that when Jesus returns He will vindicate His people. Before all creation, He will own His bride as His and see to it that she is honored.

How glorious is the Bridegroom and what glories await the Bride! Draw comfort from these assurances and heed the exhortations to forget and worship!

February 14

The Therapy of Thanks in the Thick of Things

(A Reading from Roger)

From God's Word, the Bible...

And as day was about to dawn, Paul implored them all to take food, saying, "Today is the fourteenth day you have waited and continued without food, and eaten nothing. Therefore I urge you to take nourishment, for this is for your survival, since not a hair will fall from the head of any of you." And when he had said these things, he took bread and gave thanks to God in the presence of them all; and when he had broken it he began to eat. Then they were all encouraged, and also took food themselves.

Acts 27:33-36

In Acts 27 we find the Apostle Paul "in the thick of things." You know what I mean by the thick of things: serious trouble or dire circumstances! I wonder if the phrase is an offshoot of "the thick of battle," which refers to that part of battle in which the heaviest fighting occurs.

But back to Paul; a prisoner of the Roman government, he was sailing to Rome to stand trial before Caesar (Acts 26:32). The charge leveled against him was sedition, that is, the inciting of rebellion against the government (Acts 24:5-6).

That would seem to be trouble enough. But Paul's trouble was only beginning. His ship encountered a "tempestuous head wind," which was called "Euroclydon," that is, a northeasterly wind.

This storm was so severe, that Luke, the author of Acts, says: ". . .we were exceedingly tempest-tossed" (v. 18), and ". . .no small tempest beat on us" (v. 20).

To make things worse, this storm continued for several days, two weeks to be exact! (v. 33).

The sailors had given up all hope. But in the midst of their despair, Paul came to offer encouragement and hope. One of the ways in which he did this was by giving them food.

Now here is a remarkable thing—in that setting of crisis, fear, confusion and exhaustion, Paul did not merely offer food. He first "gave thanks to God in the presence of them all" (v. 35).

If there has ever been a time in which the giving of thanks might seem to be out of place, this was it!

Paul could have said: "The men are preoccupied with the storm. There is no point in giving thanks." Or he could have said: "The men are in no mood to have religion crammed down their throats." Or he could have said: "The men will think I am crazy to thank God for food with this storm going on. Why thank God for the food when He won't stop the storm?"

But Paul expressed thanks just the same. It was a situation that would seem to call for bitterness, anger and skepticism, but Paul used it as an occasion for thanksgiving.

Why did he do it? Some would say it was mere force of habit, that Paul was observing his routine without thinking. That won't work. Paul was far too thoughtful, far too devoted to Christ, and far too genuine than to do this out of habit. This was a sincere expression of worship to God.

By doing this, Paul was declaring his conviction that God is with us in every situation. There would be no need to pray if God were not there to hear the prayer.

Paul was also registering his firm belief that every good thing comes from God, even something as common as food, and that we owe thanks to Him. We must be thankful for the big things (v. 24), but we must not think that we exhaust our responsibility in so doing. We must also be thankful for the small things. By the way, if we are always thankful for small blessings, we will never fail to be thankful for large blessings.

Paul was also showing his companions that we are blessed even while we are burdened.

And what resulted from Paul's simple act of thanksgiving? Luke says ". . . they were all encouraged. . ." (v. 36).

Thankfulness never fails to leave a favorable impression. Sourness also leaves an impression but never a favorable one.

So let's make up our minds that we can go through life humbly grateful or grumbly hateful, and let's make it our business to choose the former.

With all his difficulties Paul was a grateful man. Do you wonder what he would say if he were asked to name the thing for which he was most grateful? I think he would say: "Thanks be to God for His indescribable gift" (2 Cor. 8:9). That gift, of course, is Christ and the eternal life we can receive through Him.

Be grateful for all God's gifts, and don't ever fail to be grateful for the greatest of His gifts.

I Want to Hear Bert Wilson Pray Again

(A Reading from Roger)

From God's Word, the Bible...

Confess your trespasses to one another, and pray for one another, that you may be healed. The effective, fervent prayer of a righteous man avails much. Elijah was a man with a nature like ours, and he prayed earnestly that it would not rain; and it did not rain on the land for three years and six months. And he prayed again, and the heaven gave rain, and the earth produced its fruit.

James 5:16-18

Before I began serving as a pastor (at age sixteen), I was a member of Vanburensburg Baptist Church in Vanburensburg, Illinois. It is likely that there are more letters in the church's name than there were members of the church.

One of the members was Bert Wilson. When I first got acquainted with Bert, he was already well advanced in years. I remember him as being very warm, kind, and humble.

The thing I remember most about Bert was his praying. Our dear pastor, Ernest Flowers—himself a wonderful Christian man—would often call on Bert to lead the congregation in prayer.

Our little church did not have pews. We had what we called theater seats. But they weren't plush, cushioned seats. They had wooden backs and wooden seats, and when we got up the seats would make a rather loud clacking noise. When the pastor called on Bert to pray, those seats would clack as members across the tiny building rose, not to stand during the prayer, but rather to kneel on the hardwood floor.

Everyone knew what to expect when Bert led in prayer. It would not be brief, light, and breezy. It would last from ten to fifteen minutes, and it would be earnest, heartfelt, and moving. It taught me that there is such a thing as laying hold of God in prayer. By the way, in the four or five years that I was a member of that church, I never heard anyone complain about the time Bert took to pray. If there had been any complaints about Bert's praying, I think they would have been along the lines of it being too brief. How that man prayed! And how time seemed to stand still when he prayed! Many in the congregation would find themselves lost in wonder, love, and praise when Bert prayed, and it was not at all unusual to hear people weeping during the prayer and to see tear-stained cheeks when it was over.

Bert was short in physical stature, but he was a spiritual giant. His prayers reminded us of the sovereignty and majesty of God and of His marvelous saving love—love that sent His Son to die on the cross for a world of unlovely, unworthy, undeserving sinners.

The trend in churches in recent years has been running against Bert Wilson. He would undoubtedly be told that prayer can't take too much time and can't be quite so serious. It seems these days that we are bent on making God small and casual. We dress casually, we pray casually, we preach casually, and we hurry to get through. The God of our day is smiling, benign, and user-friendly. His primary purpose seems to be to help us cope with life's difficulties and to manage our busy schedules. After it is all over, we might allow ourselves in an infrequent moment of deep reflection to wonder why God doesn't thrill our souls. We should not expect to get a big thrill from a little God. If we insist on making God little, we will get little in return. Bert prayed to a big God.

Serious times call for serious praying. These are serious times. Where are those who are seriously praying?

I am not Bert Wilson's equal in praying. My praying must sound in God's ears like the babbling of an infant compared to Bert's. But I do pray, and one of my prayers these days is this: Lord give us more Bert Wilsons.

I have many precious memories from my youth, but if someone were to ask me to choose one thing to relive, I think I would say: I want to hear Bert Wilson pray again.

Hard Thoughts About God

(A Reading from Martyn)

From God's Word, the Bible...

"For the kingdom of heaven is like a man traveling to a far country, who called his own servants and delivered his goods to them. And to one he gave five talents, to another two, and to another one, to each according to his own ability; and immediately he went on a journey. Then he who had received the five talents went and traded with them, and made another five talents. And likewise he who had received two gained two more also. But he who had received one went and dug in the ground, and hid his lord's money. After a long time the lord of those servants came and settled accounts with them."

Matthew 25:14-19

(Read Matthew 25:14-30 for this meditation.)

Jesus told the Parable of the Talents in Matthew 25:14-30. The first two servants in the parable made use of what their master entrusted to them and earned more talents for him. The third servant hid his master's money in the ground. When called to account, he defended his actions by saying, "Lord, I knew you to be a hard man."

There are many like the servant in this parable who have hard thoughts about God.

Many people perceive God to be harsh and demanding. When some think of God they believe Him to be exclusively a Lawgiver and a Judge. He is one who makes constant demands of us and who can never be pleased. This was Martin Luther's view of God before his glorious conversion.

Many think of God as one whose requirements of us far outweigh and surpass His gifts to us. They consider Him to be like Pharaoh who withheld straw from the Hebrews but still required them to produce the same number of bricks.

Another "hard thought" a lot of people have is that God is quick to punish and slow to reward. There are those who think that God is not only severe in making demands upon us, but that He is also eager to punish us when we sin. Those who view God this way will find no joy in serving Him. Serving Him will be a burdensome duty motivated by fear and not love.

Another "hard thought" of God held by many is that He is distant and joyless. There are some who perceive God to be like the typical father in Victorian England. He is distant from the child and demanding of the child. The child knows him only as a strict disciplinarian. There is no sharing of joy and laughter between father and child. There is only distance and coldness.

As God's people, we must beware of holding such hard thoughts about God. It is true that God is our Lawgiver and Judge. It is true that His Law makes demands upon us. But we must never forget that God is bountiful and generous, and pours out blessings upon us. The servant in this parable accused the master of expecting to reap where he has not sown. In pouring out His goodness, God does just the opposite. He sows kindness and blessings where He reaps no praise, thanks, or worship in return. He fills sinners with food who never thank Him for it. He gives life and breath to many who despise Him. How good God is!

Contrary to the hard thoughts about Him, God delights in rewarding His people. He does not forget faithful service rendered to Him, and it is His delight to reward His people for their obedience. The great marvel is that we would not obey God or perform any acts for His glory apart from Him working in us. So He grants us grace to obey Him and then graciously rewards our obedience. Oh, the goodness of God!

In his commentary on this passage, Alexander Maclaren wrote:

> My heart says to me many a time, "God's laws are hard; God's judgment is strict. God requires what you cannot give. Crouch before Him and be afraid." And my faith says, "Get thee behind me, Satan! He that spared not His own Son...how shall He not with Him also freely give us all things?" The cross of Christ is the answer to the slander of the giving God.[3]

The Bible also makes it clear that God is not like a distant, emotionless father. Rather, His heart is full of warmth, love, and joy. There is no joy like God's, and He loves to give expression to His joy. He desires for His people to be near Him and to share in His joy for all eternity.

Child of God, are you guilty of thinking your Father in heaven to be harsh and severe? Have you lost your joy in serving Him? Do you view Him as more of a taskmaster than a joyful Father who loves to be with His children? Meditate on the goodness, the kindness, the joy, the love of God. Ponder again the cross of Christ and delight yourself in the Lord and in His service!

3 Alexander Maclaren, *Expositions of Holy Scripture: St Matthew, Chaps. XVIII to XXVIII*, Baker Book House, Grand Rapids, MI, 1974, p. 209.

My Sanctified Dog, Gus

(A Reading from Tim)

From God's Word, the Bible...

. . .Grow in the grace and knowledge of our Lord and Savior Jesus Christ. To Him be the glory both now and forever. Amen.

2 Peter 3:18

I miss our morning conversations the most. Every morning I would go outside to see my dogs. While they were both happy to see me, Gus expressed his joy in a much more vocal way. It was almost as if he were singing to me with a "roo, roo, roo" type of sound that must have annoyed the neighbors. Sometimes I had to go back into the house just to get him to stop.

He was always thrilled to see me at any time of the day, but only in the mornings was I greeted in such a raucous manner. I came to call it my morning conversation with Gus. It was like he had been waiting all night to see me, and he simply wanted to tell my how his night had been.

I got Gus when he was just a puppy, probably only about three weeks old. He and his momma, who was half golden retriever, were residents of the local dog pound when I came in looking for two dogs to replace those we had just lost. Gus was the only pup to survive from her litter of seven, and I took both him and his mom.

Gus (whom we named after the great Christian thinker Augustine) was a tiny little guy, fitting in the palm of my hand. He was entirely dependent upon his mother, Suzy, and when she would walk off and leave him behind, he would sit down, throw back his head, and let loose with a mournful cry. You would think his world had come to an end because his mom was a few yards away. He eventually grew to be almost twice her size, but he never stopped being her pup.

My mornings are a lot quieter now. At eleven years of age, Gus had been dealing with arthritis in his legs for some time. His condition had steadily worsened despite an increase in the pain-killing medication he was taking. It got to the place where he could hardly walk.

So we had to say goodbye. I knew for weeks that the day was coming and tried to prepare myself as best as I could. But it was still terribly difficult. He was my good and faithful friend, and a kind and gentle soul.

Through the pain he experienced late in life, Gus demonstrated to me what I grew to love most about him. The older he got and the more his legs hurt, the sweeter his disposition became. No one would have blamed him for being grumpy and sour, but that wasn't how Gus reacted. He simply loved us more and was all the more cheerful about life. Maybe he knew his days were numbered, and he wanted to make those days count.

It's probably not possible for a dog to be godly and to grow in sanctification. But all the same, Gus showed me what I must aspire to be like as I get older. Assuming that I live for at least a few more years, I'll most likely have to deal with a variety of aches and pains. Most people do. And many of them don't adjust very well. They become cranky and grouchy, and seem to take no enjoyment in their remaining days.

Gus wasn't that way at all. Just the opposite! Even until the day of his death, he was a jolly, loving, and sweet fellow, perhaps more so than he had ever been. I hope the same will one day be said of me—that as I approached death, my life reflected Christ more than ever before.

My mornings may be quieter without Gus, and I certainly miss his daily greeting. But maybe the silence will give me the opportunity to ponder the lessons he taught me and to ask myself if I'm growing in grace and love for the Lord and for His people. I pray God would make it so.

February 18

Our Need-Meeting God

(A Reading from Sylvia)

From God's Word, the Bible...

Bow down Your ear, O Lord, hear me;
For I am poor and needy.

Psalm 86:1

We are a needy people. We have physical needs. We need oxygen every minute we live. We need food and water to sustain us. We also have emotional needs such as the need for love and acceptance. As believers in Jesus Christ we know about spiritual needs. We need a Savior who has forgiven our sins and given us His righteousness. We need God's grace and strength to face the trials of this life.

Even though we are a very needy people, we are not always conscious of our needs. But when difficulties and trials come our way we realize how needy we are, and how much we need God's help.

This was driven home to our family when our five-year-old grandson, Noah, was diagnosed with leukemia. We became keenly aware of our neediness. We needed God's healing grace for Noah. His parents needed wisdom for many decisions that suddenly had to be made. They desperately needed God's strength and peace to deal with their young child's suffering and the realization that he was facing three years of treatments with ugly side effects. Noah's two older siblings were needy as well. They needed understanding and patience to deal with the upheaval this journey would bring to their lives.

And then there was little Noah and his great needs. Yes, he needed healing. But in order for that healing to come about, he needed an abundant measure of courage and strength to face three years of needles, medical procedures, and the horrible side effects of the poisonous chemotherapy drug surging through his small body. How could one so young deal with all this—so much of which he could not even understand?

The answer to that question came early in Noah's leukemia journey. After two weeks of in-patient care at St. Jude Children's Hospital followed by several weeks of living in Memphis, Tennessee, to be near the hospital for daily out-patient treatments, Noah was able to return home.

Then began the hour-and-fifteen-minute weekly trips from home to St. Jude for blood work, doctor visits, and chemo treatments. Early in the routine of one of those Monday trips as our daughter-in-law was driving, she heard singing coming from the back seat. She listened closely to hear five-year-old Noah singing:

I need Thee, O I need Thee;
Every hour I need Thee!
O bless me now, my Savior,
I come to Thee.

Even at such a young age Noah seemed to realize his need for God's help. That was the answer to the question of how one so young and so needy could deal with this difficult journey that had been thrust upon him. And God in His grace met Noah's need. The treatments resulted in a cure for Noah. And with God's help, Noah faced his three-year-ordeal with amazing courage and strength, as did his parents and siblings.

Yes, we are indeed a needy people. But we have a need-meeting God. All thanks and praise to Him for meeting our greatest need—a Savior who provided payment for our sins so we can someday stand clean before a holy God. But thanks be to God also for meeting the many needs we have while living life in this world, and for the reminder of that coming from a five-year-old needy child.

Who Like Me?

(A Reading from Martyn)

From God's Word, the Bible...

Bless the Lord, O my soul;
And all that is within me, bless His holy name!
Bless the Lord, O my soul,
And forget not all His benefits:
Who forgives all your iniquities,
Who heals all your diseases,
Who redeems your life from destruction,
Who crowns you with lovingkindness and tender mercies,
Who satisfies your mouth with good things,
So that your youth is renewed like the eagle's.

Psalm 103:1-5
(Read the whole of Psalm 103 for this meditation.)

One of my favorite hymns is based on Psalm 103. It is entitled *Praise, My Soul, the King of Heaven*. The first stanza has these words:

Praise, my soul the King of heaven,
to His feet your tribute bring;
Ransomed, healed, restored, forgiven,
who, like me His praise should sing?
Praise Him, praise Him, praise Him, praise Him,
Praise the everlasting King.

The psalm upon which the hymn is based opens with these words:

Bless the Lord, O my soul;
And all that is within me, bless His holy name!
Bless the Lord, O my soul,
And forget not all His benefits. . .
(Psalm 103:1-2)

In the verses that follow David lists several of those benefits. That is also what the first stanza of the hymn does. It lists the benefits of being ransomed, healed, restored, forgiven. Let's consider each of these words.

The word *ransom* is similar to the word "redeem." It refers to being redeemed or delivered from sin by the payment of a price. The price that was paid for our redemption was nothing less than the blood of Jesus Christ (1 Peter 1:18-19). Psalm 103:4 reads, "Who redeems your life from destruction."

The next benefit is being *healed*. Psalm 103:3 says, "Who heals all your diseases."

Sin is a dreadful disease. It is far worse than any and all physical diseases. You would be better off to have Alzheimer's, Parkinson's, or have your body racked with cancer than to be still in the grip of sin. Sin is a terminal disease, and we are powerless to cure ourselves. The good news of the gospel is that there is healing for us in and through Jesus Christ. The miracles of physical healing He worked during His earthly ministry were meant to picture the far greater miracle of healing from the disease of sin.

The third benefit in the first stanza is being *restored*. In salvation God does a great work of restoration. He restores us to right standing with Him. He restores us to fellowship with Him. Through Christ we are reconciled to God and in Him God restores to us blessings lost in the fall and grants even greater blessings. Verse 5 of Psalm 103 says, "Who satisfies your mouth with good things, so that your youth is renewed like the eagle's." When we are saved, God restores us to a right relationship with Him, and then multiple times throughout our lives He restores and renews our strength.

The fourth benefit listed in the hymn is being *forgiven*. What a blessing this is! In Christ Jesus there is full pardon, complete forgiveness for all our sins, past, present, and future. Verse 3 of Psalm 103 says, "Who forgives all your iniquities." Verse 10 says, "He has not dealt with us according to our sins, nor punished us according to our iniquities." Verse 12 goes on to say, "As far as the east is from the west, so far has He removed our transgressions from us."

After listing these glorious benefits, the hymn writer goes on to ask, "Who like me His praise should sing?" In other words, he is saying since God has ransomed him, healed him, restored him, and forgiven him, he has great cause to praise God. Others who have been redeemed may have equal cause to praise God, but no one has greater cause to praise God. Do you believe that to be true of you, child of God? Do you believe that because of what Jesus has done for you, no one in this world has more cause to praise God than you?

A good practice for all Christians to learn is the discipline of talking to themselves. We ought to rehearse the truths of God's Word in our minds. That's what this hymn writer does. It is as if he found his soul in a cold condition and decided to give it a little coaching. He exhorts his own soul to praise the Lord. He rehearses the benefits God has bestowed upon him. He then asks his soul who should praise God more than he?

Consider memorizing this hymn and singing it on Sunday mornings as you prepare for worship. Let it be a help to you in talking to your soul and preparing yourself to praise and worship the Lord.

Dad's Old Bible

(A Reading from Roger)

From God's Word, the Bible...

Your word I have hidden in my heart,
That I might not sin against You.
Blessed are You, O Lord!
Teach me Your statutes.
With my lips I have declared
All the judgments of Your mouth.
I have rejoiced in the way of Your testimonies,
As much as in all riches.
I will meditate on Your precepts,
And contemplate Your ways.
I will delight myself in Your statutes;
I will not forget Your word.

Psalm 119:11-16

It's very old now, published in 1975. The pages are brown, and it has a musty smell. Some of the pages are loose. It is my Dad's Bible, a King James Version. I have many Bibles. I have the KJV, NKJV, ESV, NASB, HCSB, NIV, the Amplified Bible, and the Living Bible. I have Study Bibles with all sorts of detailed notes and explanations. I have plain Bibles with nothing but the Bible books themselves and four or five maps in the back. I have expensive and inexpensive Bibles. I have large-print and regular-print Bibles. I have Bibles with black, burgundy, brown, and blue covers.

But no Bible is more precious to me than Dad's Bible. As I open it I find the page where he wrote his name.

It is somewhat surprising to me that my Dad was not much of a Bible marker. I am. I underline and write notes in the margin. I seem to recall someone, after looking at all the underlinings in my Bible, asking: "If you underline the whole Bible, how is it different from one that is not underlined at all?"

My Dad did underline a little. One of the few verses, interestingly enough, comes from the tiny prophecy of Obadiah: "But upon mount Zion shall be deliverance, and there shall be holiness; and the house of Jacob shall possess their possessions" (v. 17).

I'm not sure why that verse was so special to Dad. My guess is that it made him look forward to that glorious day in which the people of God will possess all that God has promised to give them.

One of the underlined verses in the New Testament is John 6:29—"Jesus answered and said unto them, This is the work of God, that ye believe on him whom he hath sent."

This verse points out the importance of believing in the Lord Jesus Christ. While still a young man, my father came to faith in Christ. He loved and served the Lord Jesus. It is no surprise that one of his underlined verses is Philippians 1:21—"For to me to live is Christ, and to die is gain."

Another verse he marked in Philippians is Paul's warning to rejoice in Christ and put no confidence in the flesh (Phil. 3:3).

One of the more heavily marked sections is in Paul's first letter to the Thessalonians: "For this we say unto you by the word of the Lord, that we which are alive and remain unto the coming of the Lord shall not prevent them which are asleep. For the Lord himself shall descend from heaven with a shout, with the voice of the archangel, and with the trump of God: and the dead in Christ shall rise first: Then we which are alive and remain shall be caught up together with them in the clouds to meet the Lord in the air: and so shall we ever be with the Lord" (1 Thess. 4:15-17).

Dad died on August 4, 1985. His body lies alongside my mother's in little Greenhill Cemetery, just outside Vanburensburg, Illinois. His soul is already with the Lord, and now his body waits for the sound of the trumpet, the voice of the archangel, and the shout of Jesus. That body will then spring from the grave, will be instantaneously changed into a body just like the resurrection body of Jesus (Phil. 3:21), will be re-joined to his soul, and he will soul and body be forever with the Lord. How do I know these things to be true? They are all right there in Dad's old Bible.

Though the cover is worn, And the pages are torn,
And though places bear traces of tears,
Yet more precious than gold, Is the Book, worn and old,
That can shatter and scatter my fears.

When I prayerfully look, In the precious old Book,
Many pleasures and treasures I see;
Many tokens of love, From the Father above,
Who is nearest and dearest to me.

This old Book is my guide, This a friend by my side,
It will lighten and brighten my way;
And each promise I find, Soothes and gladdens my mind
As I read it and heed it today.
(AUTHOR UNKNOWN)

Getting the "Hallelujah!" Back (1)

(A Reading from Roger)

From God's Word, the Bible...

Thanks be to God for His indescribable gift!

2 Corinthians 9:15

When was the last time you let out a good hearty Hallelujah? For that matter, when was the last time you silently cried Hallelujah? The Hallelujah, along with the Amen, seems to have been carried off and buried in the cemetery of good Christian words. Did it die from lack of use?

The word Hallelujah, meaning "God be praised," is a word that was intended to express the thrill believers get from their God. It could be used in reference to all the works and wonders of God, but it is never more fitting than when it is used in connection with the redeeming death of the Lord Jesus Christ.

Philip Bliss used the word in the highest and best way:

"Man of sorrows," what a name, For the Son of God who came
Ruined sinners to reclaim! Hallelujah! What a Savior!

Bearing shame and scoffing rude, In my place condemned He stood,
Seal'd my pardon with His blood; Hallelujah! What a Savior!

Lifted up was He to die, "It is finished," was His cry,
Now in heav'n exalted high, Hallelujah! What a Savior!

When He comes, our glorious King, All His ransomed home to bring,
Then anew this song we'll sing, Hallelujah! What a Savior!

What will it take for the church to get her Hallelujahs back? For one thing, she must think deeply again about Bliss' phrase "ruined sinners." No one can ever truly rejoice in salvation until he has known himself to be a ruined sinner. To be a sinner is to stand guilty before the holy God. It is to be guilty of breaking His laws. And the "ruined" part? That means any chance of ever standing acceptably in the presence of God is gone—ruined! We are guilty sinners, and there is nothing we can do to remedy our situation.

On top of that the church must think in depth about those words ". . .the Son of God who came."

Here we are in our sins with no way of helping ourselves, but God did something for us. He sent His Son, the Lord Jesus, to this earth to "reclaim" sinners. Can it be that God could care enough for sinners to send His Son?

And getting "Hallelujah" back means thinking through what Jesus had to endure in order to save sinners. Bliss gets at a tiny portion of it in the phrase "bearing shame and scoffing rude." After He was taken into custody, the Lord Jesus had to bear the vilest mockery imaginable. Shame and scoffing were heaped upon Him. Then He was "lifted up" to die on the cross. Why did He endure all the shame and suffering? Let Bliss answer: "In my place condemned He stood."

Everything Jesus endured was that which sinners deserve to endure. Every evil thing that came His way came because He was standing in the place of sinners. He was their substitute.

Some theologians, preachers, and church members think it is necessary to wage war on the teaching of Christ as our substitute. Some even suggest that the future wellbeing of Christianity hangs on getting rid of the notion of substitution. But it is as simple as this: if you take the substitution of Christ out of Christianity, you no longer have Christianity. And you no longer have any possibility of salvation for sinners. If you need to be up to date, you will need to get rid of substitution. Let me hang on to it and be out of date.

Biblical Christianity, and, really, there is no other kind, can be reduced to these propositions:

- I deserve hell;
- Jesus took my hell;
- Now there is nothing left for me but heaven.

But what if we take out the second proposition? What if we say that Jesus did not take our hell when He was on the cross and cried: "My God, My God, why have You forsaken Me?" (Matt. 27:46).

Yes, what then? If we know ourselves to be deserving of hell and do not say that Jesus took it on our behalf, do we not have to say that we must take it ourselves?

If we let the substitution that Bliss advocated in his hymn really soak into our brains, we won't have to worry about the *Hallelujah, what a Savior* part. Let us truly understand salvation, and the *Hallelujah* will sound inwardly or outwardly or both.

Getting the "Hallelujah!" Back (2)

(A Reading from Roger)

From God's Word, the Bible...

Seek the Lord while He may be found,
Call upon Him while He is near.
Let the wicked forsake his way,
And the unrighteous man his thoughts;
Let him return to the Lord,
And He will have mercy on him;
And to our God,
For He will abundantly pardon.

Isaiah 55:6-7

We're trying to find our way back to the word "Hallelujah," and we are doing so by looking at a well-known hymn from the pen of Philip Bliss. It can be found in some hymnals under the title *Man of Sorrows* and in others with the title *Hallelujah! What a Savior!* The former asserts that Jesus fulfilled the prophecy of Isaiah 53:6. We should not think that Jesus was a miserable and unhappy man, but He could see here the terrible effects of sin and that brought sorrow to His heart. He was also here on the serious business of receiving the penalty for sinners.

If your Hallelujah has been silenced and stifled, you will find in Bliss' hymn plenty of words and phrases to get it revived.

What blessing there is in that word "pardon"! To be pardoned is to have the just sentence—the sentence that we deserved to receive—lifted. What is the sentence for our sins? It is eternal death. By shedding His blood, Jesus secured the pardon of all who believe. That blood represents His death, and the physical blood that poured out from Him on the cross represents Him receiving the full penalty for our sins.

Get a good look at that word "pardon." Walk around it a few times. Understand the reality of your sins and what Christ did on the cross for sinners, and let the Hallelujah ring in your heart.

And what blessing there is in these words: "'It is finished,' was His cry." What Jesus did on the cross perfectly and fully purchased our salvation. There is nothing for us to add to what He did. It is ours to merely receive by faith in Him and in the work He did. When you see the enormous problem posed by the salvation of sinners and you see that Jesus solved that problem, you will cry, "Hallelujah!"

The cross on which He died is, of course, not the final word about the Lord Jesus. He sprang from His grave in glorious resurrection life and ascended to the Father in heaven. He is back in heaven in exalted glory, the object of the praises of the angels. But He is not back in heaven now in the same way that He was before. He has carried the humanity that He took at Bethlehem back to heaven with Him. And the fact that He is there in resurrected humanity is the guarantee that all who believe in Him will follow Him into heaven in resurrected humanity. Now, that will make you shout, "Hallelujah! What a Savior!"

If Hallelujah is still fading in our hearts and dying on our tongues, we can surely get it back by savoring this verse:

When He comes, our glorious King,
All His ransomed home to bring,
Then anew this song we'll sing,
Hallelujah! what a Savior!

The Lord Jesus will return from heaven with a shout, the voice of an archangel, and a blast from the trumpet of God. He will bring with Him the souls of all believers who have died, and He will raise their bodies from their graves. Those resurrected bodies will be rejoined to those souls, and those believers who are still alive will be instantaneously changed and caught up to meet the Lord in the air (1 Thess. 4:13-18).

From there the Lord Jesus will lead His people into the glory of a new heaven and a new earth (Rev. 21 and 22). There we will see the magnificent sweep of redemption's plan, and we will marvel at it all. We will be amazed and astounded beyond words at a plan that was born in eternity past in the mind and heart of the triune God, that caught us up as it swept through human history, and finally dropped us on heaven's shore. There our Hallelujahs will abound and will never diminish and never decrease.

In these days, many in the church are striving for relevance. In so doing, they are focusing on helping people cope with their problems and helping them manage the challenges of life. The question that ought to be pounding in our heads is this: in our quest to make Christianity relevant, have we made it small? We need not expect a small Christianity to thrill us. The hymn of Philip Bliss lets us see how big true Christianity is, and urges us when we have seen it to shout, "Hallelujah!"

Seeing from Heaven's Glory with Heaven's Eyes

(A Reading from Sylvia)

From God's Word, the Bible...

For now we see in a mirror, dimly, but then face to face. Now I know in part, but then I shall know just as I also am known.

Therefore we do not lose heart. Even though our outward man is perishing, yet the inward man is being renewed day by day. For our light affliction, which is but for a moment, is working for us a far more exceeding and eternal weight of glory, while we do not look at the things which are seen, but at the things which are not seen. For the things which are seen are temporary, but the things which are not seen are eternal.

1 Corinthians 13:12; 2 Corinthians 4:16-18

In the small country church I attended in my childhood years, we often sang the hymn *Farther Along*. This hymn, sometimes attributed to W.B. Stevens and sometimes to W.A. Fletcher, came to mean so very much to me because of a horrible tragedy in our community.

I was nine years old. I can still see the six caskets at the graveside service. The closed caskets were lined up from the largest to smallest. Inside the largest casket was the body of a mother. The next casket held the body of her teenage daughter, followed by four younger children. This mother and her five children had died in a house fire. They lived in the little community where my family attended church, and the children had sometimes attended our church.

The family was extremely poor. The husband and father had abandoned the family so the mother was rearing the children with the help of her father who lived with them in their tiny house. The night of the fire, the grandfather and two boys, one of whom was my age, were able to escape the burning house. But the mother and the other five children perished in the fire.

I remember the perplexity of the godly people in my church family, including my parents. There were no words to express the depth of this tragedy and the sorrow it brought to all our hearts. It was so hard to understand why a family that had so much hardship had to come to such a tragic end. But there could be no understanding it—at least not in this life. But our faith in God assured us that we would understand by and by. So as people from our church and the community gathered in the cemetery that cold day in 1955, a group from our church sang these words:

Tempted and tried we're oft made to wonder
Why it should be thus all the day long,
While there are others living about us,
Never molested, though in the wrong.

(Refrain)
Farther along we'll know all about it,
Farther along we'll understand why;
Cheer up my brother, live in the sunshine,
We'll understand it all by and by.

As verse two was sung I remember how I grieved for the surviving members of this family as I thought about how lonely and drear their future days would be.

When death has come and taken our loved ones
It leaves our home so lonely and drear,
Then do we wonder why others prosper
Living so wicked year after year.

The last verse and chorus was an expression of our hope in spite of our inability to understand:

When we see Jesus, coming in glory,
When He comes from His home in the sky,
Then we shall meet Him in that bright mansion,
We'll understand it all by and by.

Decades later, the scene of six caskets of descending size lined up in a cemetery has never left me. I have never heard *Farther Along* sung or played without that scene rushing back to my mind.

Farther along we'll know all about it,
Farther along we'll understand why;
Cheer up my brother, live in the sunshine,
We'll understand it all by and by.

God's people often yearn to have the tragedies of this life explained here and now, but we do not get all the explanations we desire. We must wait for that time in which we enter heaven's glory. Then we will see with heaven's eyes. And then, at last, we will understand. Farther along!

The New Dress

(A Reading from Sylvia)

From God's Word, the Bible...

For He made Him who knew no sin to be sin for us, that we might become the righteousness of God in Him.

2 Corinthians 5:21

It was a blue print, shirt-waist style dress that I can still picture decades later. But my mother's reaction to it took me completely by surprise. I was thirteen years old and had just returned from a trip to Texas. The trip was an eighth grade graduation present from my aunt.

My aunt and her daughter had previously lived in Texas where my uncle's family resided but had moved back home to Illinois after my uncle died. Now two years later they were taking a vacation trip to Texas to visit relatives and invited me to go along.

I had been given a little money by my parents to spend on the trip. I also had some graduation gift money and the money I had been saving for weeks in anticipation of this trip. Of course I would spend some of that on souvenirs for my parents and four younger brothers. It would be unthinkable to return home without bringing gifts for my family.

Once we arrived in Texas, every place we stopped had souvenirs for sale. I picked out inexpensive trinkets for my dad and brothers. But for my mother I had something different in mind. I wanted to buy her a dress.

My dad was a hardworking but struggling farmer. And with five children, there was barely enough money to provide the necessities. My mother, like most mothers, always sacrificed her own wants and often her needs in order to provide for her children. A new dress was a luxury Mother rarely allowed herself to enjoy. She always saw to it that I had a new dress for Easter, but that didn't leave any money for a new dress for her.

Assessing the amount of money I had to spend on this trip, I came up with a plan. If I would buy some inexpensive gifts for my dad and brothers and spent sparingly on myself, I would probably have enough money to buy Mom a dress. And that is exactly what I did. My aunt took me to a dress shop where I took my time looking at the dresses and finally picked out the dress that I thought would be perfect for Mom.

Upon my return home I proudly presented my family members with their gifts. My dad and brothers were pleased with their trinkets, but when my mother opened the box containing the dress she began to cry—tears of surprise and joy. I expected her to be pleased, but I had no idea she would react with such emotion. She wore the new dress to church the next Sunday and many Sundays afterward.

As I was thinking recently about this event from my childhood, I thought about another kind of dress—the robe of righteousness given to us when we receive Jesus Christ as our Lord and Savior. I recalled the words in Isaiah 61:10:

I will greatly rejoice in the LORD,
My soul shall be joyful in my God;
For He has clothed me with the garments of salvation,
He has covered me with the robe of righteousness...

How marvelous is this garment of salvation, the robe of righteousness. It has been provided as a free gift from God. In order to be acceptable to God we must be righteous, meaning perfect. Because we can never be perfect by our own efforts, our gracious God provided a righteousness for us through the Lord Jesus Christ.

This priceless gift of righteousness should bring great joy to us, not only when we are first saved, but throughout the rest of our lives. In fact the joy of our salvation should increase all the more as we grow spiritually and as our knowledge of the plan of redemption increases. Our joy will reach its pinnacle when we stand before God at the end of time, and in the words of Edward Mote we are

Dressed in His righteousness alone,
Faultless to stand before the throne.
(FROM THE HYMN, THE SOLID ROCK)

My mother's new dress eventually faded and wore out, but thank God our garment of salvation, the robe of righteousness, will never fade or wear out but will clothe us throughout eternity.

The Wonderful Cross

(A Reading from Roger)

From God's Word, the Bible...

But God demonstrates His own love toward us, in that while we were still sinners, Christ died for us.

Romans 5:8

The Apostle Paul was a cross-lover. He loved the cross of Christ. To him, the cross was the most wonderful thing in all of human history.

Do you understand Paul? Are you a cross-lover? If you were asked to name the one thing that is more wonderful to you than anything else, what would you say?

Every Christian loves the cross of Christ, but we all need to love it more.

I am asking you to think with me about that cross. In particular, I am asking you to think with me about this question: what makes the cross of Christ so wonderful?

My first answer to that question is this: it is wonderful because of the person who died there.

It isn't enough to merely say Jesus of Nazareth was on that cross. Nor is it enough to say a great teacher was there, or a great moral example was there.

You have never said enough about Jesus until you say He was God in human flesh. Someone has estimated that 60 billion people have occupied planet earth. The Lord Jesus can be described as 1 in 60 billion. I am saying that He is in a class by Himself. No one else is like Him—fully God, fully man—the God-man!

Are you wishing you could know the truth about Jesus? You can. These things tell you everything you need to know about Him:

- the prophecies He fulfilled
- the miracles He performed
- the words He spoke
- the lives He changed
- the grave He conquered

My second answer to that question is this: it is wonderful because of what He did there.

Jesus was not only a special person; He was on that cross to die a special death—a death such as no one before had ever died or anyone since.

It is never enough to think of Jesus' death in mere physical terms. Yes, He died physically, but there was much more to it than that.

Jesus was on that cross to receive the penalty for sinners. What is that penalty? It is eternal separation from God. Jesus bore that penalty. He experienced an eternity's worth of separation from God there. That's why He cried, "My God, My God, why have You forsaken Me?" (Matt. 27:46).

If you ask me how Jesus in the six hours He was on the cross could receive an eternity's worth of the wrath of God, I would say: because He was an infinite person, He could bear in a finite amount of time an infinite amount of wrath.

Paul, the cross-lover, says in Romans 3:25 that Jesus is the propitiation for our sins. That word propitiation means He appeased or satisfied the wrath of God on behalf of sinners.

Have you ever wondered why we tell people to trust in Jesus and what He did on the cross for their eternal salvation? The Romans crucified thousands of men. Why do we say look to this one man hanging on this one cross? It is because He was a special man dying a special kind of death.

Here is my final answer to that question: it is wonderful because of what put that special man there to do that special work.

The love of God put Jesus on that cross—the love of God for unworthy, undeserving sinners. Our calling is not to understand that love—it is far too great for that—but to rejoice in it and to worship the One who has loved us.

Could we with ink the ocean fill,
And were the skies of parchment made,
Were every stalk on earth a quill,
And every man a scribe by trade;
To write the love of God above
Would drain the ocean dry;
Nor could the scroll contain the whole,
Tho' stretched from sky to sky.
(Frederick M. Lehman, The Love of God)

God's Prescription for an Age-Old Malady

(A Reading from Martyn)

FROM GOD'S WORD, THE BIBLE...

Do not fret because of evildoers,
Nor be envious of the workers of iniquity.
For they shall soon be cut down like the grass,
And wither as the green herb.
Trust in the LORD, and do good;
Dwell in the land, and feed on His faithfulness.
Delight yourself also in the LORD,
And He shall give you the desires of your heart.

PSALM 37:1-4
(Read the whole of Psalm 37 for this meditation.)

As we travel through this life there are times when our souls are afflicted by various maladies. One of the things that can lead us into a dark season of the soul is the fact that the wicked often prosper in this life. God's people seek to honor Him, yet we often seem to fail and have little to show for our efforts. The wicked, on the other hand, give no thought to God yet seem to always meet with success. They are often rich and prosperous. They often occupy positions of leadership and influence. This malady of being discouraged when the wicked prosper has been around a long time. It is still with us today.

In Psalm 37 God has a prescription to cure this malady. This prescription involves some things we must not do and some things we must do.

The first thing we must not do is fret (v. 1). We are not to get worked up and worry ourselves over the prosperity of the wicked. Even though the wicked prosper and bring their schemes to pass, we are not to fret over it.

The second thing we must not do is become envious (v. 1). The people of God should never desire to trade places with the wicked. Verse 2 tells us why we should not envy the wicked.

For they shall soon be cut down like the grass,
And wither as the green herb.

They may be prospering for now, but their prosperity will be short-lived.

The third thing we must not do is give way to anger and wrath (v. 8). When the wicked seem to be triumphing we must guard against becoming angry with God. Are you ever tempted to say in anger: "Why doesn't God do something about...?"

These verses also give us a positive side to this prescription. They tell us two things we must do.

First, we must look up. We must get our eyes off the godless and fix our eyes upon God. Verse 3 tells us to "Trust in the LORD." Trust Him and never forget that He is in control of all things. Verse 3 goes on to say, "and do good." Don't be taken up with what the wicked are doing. Be taken up with what God has given you to do. Verse 4 tells us to delight ourselves in the Lord. The energy spent worrying about the godless could better be spent delighting in God. We are further told in verse 7 to "rest in the LORD." Rest in knowing that every promise God has made about the triumph of His kingdom will be fulfilled. Wait patiently for God to act. Rest in knowing that the governing of all things is in the best possible hands.

Secondly, we must look ahead. We are to look to the future and know that a great change is coming. Verse 9 tells us, "evildoers shall be cut off; but those who wait on the LORD, they shall inherit the earth."

The same idea is expanded upon in verses 10 and 11. When you are tempted to despair over the prosperity of the wicked remember that phrase in verse 10, "for yet a little while." The wicked may seem to be having their day, but their time will soon come to an end. Look to the future and know that there will be no peace for the wicked, and there will be nothing but peace for the saints of God. When the wicked are gone and forgotten, the righteous will be forever enjoying the earth they have inherited and delighting themselves in the abundance of peace.

If you are afflicted by the malady of being discouraged by wicked people who seem to always succeed, read Psalm 37 and meditate deeply upon it. It is God's prescription for this age-old malady.

February 27

The Ups and Downs of Faith

(A Reading from Roger)

From God's Word, the Bible...

Then the word of the Lord came to Jeremiah, saying, "Behold, I am the Lord, the God of all flesh. Is there anything too hard for Me?"

Jeremiah 32:26-27
(Read the whole of Jeremiah 32 for this meditation.)

These were terrible days for the city of Jerusalem. She was surrounded by the Babylonian army. And they were terrible days for Jeremiah. He was in prison (v.2).

While Jeremiah was whiling away his time in jail, the Lord told him to expect a visit from his cousin Hanamel. Hanamel owned a field in nearby Anathoth, and he wanted to sell it to Jeremiah. Perhaps Hanamel had figured a way to get out of town, and he needed a little spending money.

The presence of the Babylonian army outside the city had caused all commerce to cease in Jerusalem. But Hanamel figured his weird cousin Jeremiah might take the field off his hands.

The Lord told Jeremiah to do exactly that, and Jeremiah did. He paid Hanamel the seventeen shekels he was asking for the field and had two deeds properly and legally prepared.

Here we see Jeremiah functioning as a child of God ought to function—in faith. He listened to God, believed God, and obeyed God.

This deal should have made sense to Jeremiah. He had been preaching two things for a long time: (1) the people of Jerusalem would be taken captive by the Babylonians; (2) after seventy years the people would be released from their captivity in Babylon (29.10,14; 30.8,10-11,18; 31.8,10,16-17,23-28)

So Jeremiah should have understood that in buying this field, he was providing something that his descendants could use. But he began to waver. He did not doubt the first part of his message. He believed the captivity would take place. As he looked out the window, he could see the Babylonian army!

But for some reason he seemed to doubt the second part of his message, namely, that the Jews would be released. So he began to question God. Why did God want him to act as if there was a future for the Jews when their circumstances seemed to suggest otherwise?

The Babylonians were so strong, and the Jews were so weak! Did it not make more sense to believe that the Babylonian captivity would be the final word for the Jews?

In the midst of his bout with doubt, Jeremiah did a very wise thing. He prayed! (v. 16). Let this be a lesson to us! When we have difficulties on every hand and our faith is weak, let us pray! Let us tell the Lord all about it! Matthew Henry says: "Prayer is the salve for every sore."

The Lord responded to Jeremiah's prayer of doubt. Here is the very first thing the Lord said to him: "Behold, I am the LORD, the God of all flesh. Is there anything too hard for Me?" (v. 26).

This question, Phillip Ryken suggests, contains "an ounce of rebuke and a pound of grace."

Yes, there is rebuke here. Knowing as he did about the greatness of God, Jeremiah should not have allowed himself to slip into doubt. But there is more grace here than rebuke. Any time the Lord reminds us of His greatness, He is being gracious to us.

God was promising two things regarding the people of Jerusalem: they would be taken captive to Babylon and they would eventually be restored to their land. In other words, God was promising both calamity and hope. Jeremiah did not doubt the calamity part. He could see the Babylonians outside the city. He did, however, doubt the hope part.

We are often like Jeremiah. In light of the greatness of our sins, it is often easier for us to believe that God will judge than that He will forgive. We find ourselves wondering how it's possible for a holy God to forgive such great sinners. God says the same to us that He said to Jeremiah: Nothing is impossible with Him. That includes forgiveness. Forgiveness for our sins might seem impossible to us, but God found a way. That way is His Son, Jesus, dying on the cross.

Let's come away from Jeremiah's experience asking ourselves:

- Do we believe God's Word even when it seems foolish to do so?
- Do we tell the Lord about our doubts and uncertainties?
- Do we really believe that nothing is impossible with God, even the forgiveness of our sins?

Lord, Help Me to Spaffordize

(A Reading from Roger)

From God's Word, the Bible...

For our light affliction, which is but for a moment, is working for us a far more exceeding and eternal weight of glory, while we do not look at the things which are seen, but at the things which are not seen. For the things which are seen are temporary, but the things which are not seen are eternal.

2 Corinthians 4:17-18

You've never heard the word "spaffordize"? There's a reason for that. I just now made it up. It is based on the name of a man who lived many years ago—Horatio G. Spafford. To "spaffordize," I suggest, is to respond to brutal circumstances the way he did.

The date was November 22, 1873. On its way to England, the ship *Ville du Havre* was struck by another vessel and sank. Many people—226—lost their lives, including the four young daughters of Horatio and Anna Spafford. Anna was also on the ship but survived. The loss of their daughters followed the death from scarlet fever of their four-year-old son two years earlier.

Upon learning of the tragedy, Spafford himself set sail for England to be with his wife. His voyage took him over the place where his daughters had died, and it gave him the occasion to write the hymn that has brought blessing to millions—*It is Well with My Soul.*

The words of this hymn are remarkable. There is no attempt here to deny or to soften the pain of the trial. Quite the opposite! In his second line, Spafford acknowledges his crushing grief: "When sorrows like sea billows roll. . . "

The hymn powerfully affirms two truths in which every Christian can find refuge in the midst of the most heart-breaking trials.

The first truth is this: the greatness of the burden does not destroy the greatness of the blessing.

Though Satan should buffet, tho' trials should come,
Let this blest assurance control,
That Christ has regarded my helpless estate,
And hath shed His own blood for my soul.

The Christian may be broken, beaten, and battered, but he is also blessed.

In the midst of the most trying circumstances, he can always say: "Yes, but. . ." He says "Yes" regarding the trial. Yes, it hurts. Yes, it breaks my heart. Yes, the tears flow. Yes, the questions abound. Then he adds the word "but"—but with it all I still enjoy the greatest of all possible blessings, that is, my salvation through Christ. No earthly ill, no matter how severe and heart-wrenching, can ever deprive me of that blessing. The things of this world—families, friends, health, possessions, pleasures—are not secure. Salvation through Christ is. So the believer can say: "It is well, it is well with my soul," and nothing can ever keep such a person from saying it. And it is not just a matter of saying it but rather rejoicing in it with worshipful amazement:

My sin—oh the bliss of this glorious thought!
My sin, not in part but the whole,

Is nail'd to the cross, and I bear it no more,
Praise the Lord, praise the Lord, O my soul!

And the second truth? It is this: a glorious day will come when all of our sorrows and suffering will end in magnificent victory:

And, Lord, haste the day when the faith shall be sight,
The clouds be rolled back as a scroll,
The trump shall resound and the Lord shall descend,
"Even so," it is well with my soul.

Now we walk by faith, and the eye of faith is dim. The Apostle Paul tells us that we now see through a glass "darkly" (1 Cor. 13:12, KJV). But when Jesus comes, the dark glass will be removed and we shall see "face to face," that is, with clarity. On that day we will understand the things that we found so perplexing and puzzling in this life, and all will make perfect sense. T.V. Moore says there is coming a ". . .great day of final adjustment. . . in which all seeming anomalies of the present shall be fully explained and wholly removed forever."

Our faith doesn't enable us to see all that God is doing now, but it does enable us to see that coming day and to join Spafford in saying: "Lord, haste the day. . ."

Life may present you with many burdens and challenges. For me, the road has not been bump-free. But I have never had anything as crushing as what Horatio and Anna Spafford had to endure. Like yours, my journey is not complete. There may be significant hardships ahead. Whether our future problems be great or small, I pray the Lord will give grace to "spaffordize" by not letting my burdens—or your burdens—overshadow the blessing. Let us look beyond this vale of tears to that tearless day.

Can You Bear to Let Them Go?

(A Reading from Sylvia)

From God's Word, the Bible...

Deliver those who are drawn toward death,
And hold back those stumbling to the slaughter.

And He said to them, "Go into all the world and preach
the gospel to every creature.

Brethren, my heart's desire and prayer to God for Israel
is that they may be saved. . .
"How beautiful are the feet of those who preach the gospel of peace, Who
bring glad tidings of good things!"

Proverbs 24:11; Mark 16:15; Romans 10:1, 15

At a worship service I recently attended we sang the hymn, *Brethren, We Have Met to Worship* written by George Atkins. Verse two of that hymn has these words:

Brethren, see poor sinners round you
Slumbering on the brink of woe;
Death is coming, hell is moving,
Can you bear to let them go?

Many Christians appear to be answering that question in the affirmative: "Yes, we can bear to let them go." Among believers today there seems to be little concern and thus little praying and pleading for the souls of unbelievers. But I vividly remember two members of my family who demonstrated by their actions that their answer was, "No, I cannot bear to let them go." One was my Grandma Tate.

When I was in high school, I stayed all night with Grandma almost every Thursday during the school year. Grandma lived just a mile or so from the small town where I attended high school. My family lived on a farm several miles from town. On Thursdays after school, instead of riding the bus home, I walked to the home of my piano teacher for my weekly piano lesson. In order to save my parents a trip into town to get me, Grandma would pick me up after my piano lesson and take me to her house where I would spend the night.

Those Thursday nights became very special to me. There are many things I remember about those overnights, one of which was Grandma's prayer before we ate supper. She didn't just say a quick prayer to give thanks for the food. She also prayed for a husband and wife who lived across the road from her. This young couple were not Christians. Grandma's heart was burdened for their souls. I remember sitting at that table listening to her pour out her heart to God for that husband and wife to be saved. Many times her prayers for them would cause her to weep quietly. Those prayers for the salvation of her neighbors made a lasting impression on me as a teenager.

My other family member who could not bear to let unbelievers go out into eternity without Christ was my Dad, Gene Miller. He often talked about having various unbelievers on his heart. Dad would pray for them and talk to them, pleading for them to accept Christ as their Savior.

I remember two men in particular who were brothers and lived near each other and near the little church we attended. Dad "carried a burden," as he called it, for these men for years. He would go to their homes and visit them, always during our spring and fall revival meetings, but at other times during the year as well. He not only invited them to church, but also explained the plan of salvation to them and warned them of the eternal judgment to come if they did not accept Christ. Although these men did not heed Dad's warnings, they liked him and always welcomed him into their homes. And in spite of their constant rejection of Christ and their refusal to attend church, Dad kept going back.

The wife my grandma prayed for did become a Christian after Grandma died. However, as far as I know, her husband and the two men my Dad was so concerned about all went out into eternity without Jesus as their Savior.

The Bible has these instructions for us concerning unbelievers:

- We are to pray for them (Rom. 10:1).
- We are to warn them and share the gospel with them (Mark 16:15; Rom. 10:15).
- We are not to give up because of rejection (1 Thess. 2:2).
- We are to accept the fact that not all will believe (Rom. 10:16). We are not responsible for the results of our efforts. We are responsible to pray and proclaim, leaving the results to God.

Oh, that I would more closely follow the example of Dad and Grandma in saying by my actions, "No, I cannot bear to let unbelievers go to their death without my prayers and warnings" (Prov. 24:11).

A Death That Led to Life

(A Reading from Tim)

From God's Word, the Bible...

And we know that all things work together for good to those who love God, to those who are the called according to His purpose.

Romans 8:28

It was a Saturday morning. My phone rang as I sat with my family in a donut shop. I saw that the caller was Union's Dean of Students. I knew this wouldn't be good. The Dean of Students doesn't call me on a Saturday morning with tidings of comfort and joy.

"We had a student killed in a car accident last night," he said.

I didn't know the student. I had never met her. But I will be eternally grateful for her and the impact she has had on my family.

The Union University community is a tightknit group, and the death of this student was a powerful blow for the students. I hated to see them hurt. I grieved for the family and friends of the young woman.

The following Tuesday, I went to the visitation in Nashville and was struck by how tragic and senseless it all seemed. Here was a twenty-year-old girl with a bright future. What looked like a completely random accident had changed all that, leaving heartache in its wake.

I returned home the next day. As we finished dinner on that Wednesday evening, the Scripture for our family devotion time was about the crucifixion of Jesus. I used the occasion to speak to my three children about the gospel, and I used the student's death as an example of why this was such an urgent matter.

I'm sure as the student went to her classes on Friday and prepared to travel home for the weekend, she had no idea she was so close to eternity. From every indication, she was a believer in the Lord Jesus Christ, and I'm immensely grateful for that. But if she was like most of us, she wasn't giving death a single thought on that day.

I told my children that they should consider this. I told them that they could be only an unexpected car accident away from the beginning of eternity and standing before a holy God in their sins: no advocate; no mediator; the wrath of God amassed against them.

But I also told them that there is hope. Because of what the Lord Jesus accomplished through His sinless life, His sacrificial death, and His triumphant resurrection, they didn't need to fear meeting God. All they had to do was trust in Christ and His work on their behalf—to believe in the gospel—and they would be saved.

My ten-year-old son, Daniel, was especially moved as he sat and listened. Later that night, after I put the kids to bed, Daniel came out of his room with tears in his eyes, saying he wanted to be a Christian.

I talked with him about what that means, and I truly believe my precious son was converted that night. This was God's answer to the prayers we have offered for his salvation for years. Daniel later said that it was the student's death that got him to thinking seriously about the state of his soul.

The young woman's death was a terrible tragedy, and I know the lives of her loved ones will never be the same. We don't understand why God allows such things to happen, and we may never know. But we do know that God is good, that He cares for His people, and that He will work all things together for the glory of His name and the good of His people.

I do not give thanks for the tragic accident that took the life of this precious young lady. I consider it to be the fruit of the sin and rebellion that have so thoroughly ravaged God's perfect creation. I hated getting that phone call. I hated the pain and the grief the accident caused. I hate it still.

I do, however, thank God with all my heart that He is a master designer and weaver. He took the tragedy of this death and used it for something glorious and good—the salvation of my son.

The impact of this student's life didn't stop with her death, and God in His providence has forever intertwined her with my family. Though I never met her in this life, I look forward to doing so in the life to come.

A Throne Set in Heaven

(A Reading from Roger)

From God's Word, the Bible...

He who sits in the heavens shall laugh;
The Lord shall hold them in derision.
Then He shall speak to them in His wrath,
And distress them in His deep displeasure:
"Yet I have set My King
On My holy hill of Zion."

Psalm 2:4-6

I am troubled by the increasing anti-Christian sentiment that I am seeing. Hatred of Christianity seems to be growing by leaps and bounds. Ironically enough, much of it is coming from people who pride themselves on being champions of tolerance and equality.

Where can Christians find comfort and consolation in these trying and sinister times? Sometimes there is a ton of comfort in a mere ounce of words. So it is with Revelation 4:2. The Apostle John says: "Immediately I was in the Spirit; and behold, a throne set in heaven, and One sat on the throne."

When we come to the Book of Revelation, it is crucial for us to remember that it was originally given to Christians in seven churches. Those churches are identified and addressed in chapters two and three.

These people were in serious trouble. They were hated for merely being Christians. Their beliefs were not politically correct. The hatred had even led to some Christians being put to death.

Those early believers might have had moments when they wondered if there is a throne—a governing authority—anywhere in this universe or if all is a meaningless, hopeless jumble. Some might have even had moments in which they thought the governing authority of this universe is set in hell.

It must have been very reassuring for them to read John's words: ". . .behold, a throne set in heaven. . . ."

The world is not just a bundle of chaos and confusion. There is a throne, and it is in heaven. Hell does not rule. Heaven does.

If heaven is ruling, why is there so much evil in this world? This will stretch your mind to the breaking point—even the evil of this world is part of the plan! We have a tendency to take evil to mean that God has vacated the throne, but He hasn't.

No, I am not saying God is responsible for the evil in this world—not for a minute! I am saying that God in His sovereign greatness and infinite wisdom is not defeated by evil but rather uses it to bring about His purposes. Does the evil cause us to be uncomfortable? Yes, but God's primary purpose is not to make us comfortable.

In these tumultuous and threatening days, we do well to frequently remind ourselves of the story of Joseph. Was it evil for him to be hated by his brothers? Definitely. Was it evil for them to sell him into slavery? Obviously. Was it evil for him to be falsely accused by Potiphar's wife and imprisoned by Potiphar? Yes. But God had a purpose in it all (Gen. 50:20).

Then there's Daniel. Ripped away from his home in Jerusalem and transported five hundred miles to Babylon! Were those evil circumstances? They most certainly were! But God was in those circumstances and used them in a glorious way. And Daniel did not let the evil of Babylon cause him to think that God was not in control but clung to the conviction that there is a God in heaven (Dan. 2:28).

There is consolation in knowing that there is a throne in heaven. There is also consolation in that word "set." The throne John saw was set in heaven. It is not only there, but it is also not going anywhere. Men can hate it and rage against it, but they cannot destroy it. The plans of earth against heaven cannot succeed, and the plans of heaven for earth cannot fail.

Is it okay to desire peace in this chaotic world? Yes, it is. But of far greater importance is being at peace with the One who sits on the throne. How can we be at peace with God? The Book of Revelation has a lot to say about the Lamb of God. That refers, of course, to Jesus. The lamb was an animal used for sacrifice. Jesus came to this earth so He could go to the cross and there be the sacrifice for our sins. The way to be at peace with the throne of God is by faith in the Lamb of God. May God help us to join in the great chorus of Revelation 5:13:

Blessing and honor and glory and power
Be to Him who sits on the throne,
And to the Lamb, forever and ever!

THE MONTH OF MARCH

When God Blocks Our Path

... And 30 Other Bible-Based Meditations

When disappointments come our way, we may think that God has failed us and forsaken us. But Scripture assures us that such things are never the case. The Lord went with Paul even though it seemed his pathway was being blocked. He never sends His people into difficult circumstances without going with them. If God is with us in our disappointments, the thing we must do to help ourselves face those disappointments is focus on Him.

When God Blocks Our Path

FROM GOD'S WORD, THE BIBLE...

So the churches were strengthened in the faith, and increased in number daily. Now when they had gone through Phrygia and the region of Galatia, they were forbidden by the Holy Spirit to preach the word in Asia. After they had come to Mysia, they tried to go into Bithynia, but the Spirit did not permit them. So passing by Mysia, they came down to Troas. And a vision appeared to Paul in the night. A man of Macedonia stood and pleaded with him, saying, "Come over to Macedonia and help us." Now after he had seen the vision, immediately we sought to go to Macedonia, concluding that the Lord had called us to preach the gospel to them.

ACTS 16:5-10

Paul wanted to take the gospel into Asia, but he was "forbidden" by the Holy Spirit. He quickly formed a new plan, namely, to go into Bithynia. But the Spirit of God would not permit this either (v. 7). Some think the means that the Spirit used to thwart Paul's plans was sickness.

Two plans and two disappointments! So Luke, the author of Acts, tells us that Paul and his associates came down to Troas. We may well characterize Troas as the place of disappointment.

Every child of God has spent some time in Troas. We have walked its dark streets, felt the heaviness of its air, and smelled the stench of its stagnant waters.

Why does God put Troas on the itinerary for His children? Why would a loving God allow them to visit such an unpleasant place? Why is it that God seems to block our path?

We might say God has a school there in which He wants us to enroll. He sends us to Troas so He can teach us important lessons.

We don't know why it was necessary for Paul to visit Troas, but God knew. We do know this—Troas is never an accident. Our disappointments come to us in God's wise design. They wean us away from our self-sufficiency and cause us to cast ourselves in humble dependence on Him. Through our disappointments, God teaches us not to rely on our own understanding but rather to trust wholeheartedly in Him as the One who always has our best interests at heart (Prov. 3:5-6; Rom. 8:28).

When disappointments come our way, we may be inclined to think that God has failed us and forsaken us. But Scripture assures us that such things are never the case. God went with Paul to Troas. He gave Paul a vision in which a man from Macedonia "stood and pleaded" with him, saying: "Come over to Macedonia and help us" (v. 9).

The Lord never sends His people into difficult circumstances without going with them into those circumstances (Isa. 49:16; Matt. 28:20; Heb. 13:5).

If God is with us in our disappointments, the thing we must do to help ourselves face those disappointments is focus on Him. We might say that the best thing to do when facing Troas is to delight ourselves in God instead of questioning Him.

The prophet Habakkuk learned this. He was disappointed that God would use the Babylonians as His instrument to bring judgment on the people of Judah. Habakkuk learned to say:

Though the fig tree may not blossom,
Nor fruit be on the vines;
Though the labor of the olive may fail,
And the fields yield no food;
Though the flock be cut off from the fold,
And there be no herd in the stalls—
Yet I will rejoice in the LORD,
I will joy in the God of my salvation.
(HAB. 3:17-18)

It is important to note that nothing had changed in Habakkuk's circumstances when he resolved to rejoice in the Lord. The people of Judah were still sinful, and judgment was still coming. Habakkuk rejoiced because in the midst of trying circumstances, he still had God and God's salvation.

The salvation believers enjoy through Christ always puts them in a happy position—so much so that they can say they would rather have salvation with bad circumstances than not to have it with good circumstances. Believers on their worst day are always better off than unbelievers on their best day.

Troas was not a permanent place for Paul. It wasn't long until he and his company were on their way to even greater usefulness for God. God's people never enjoy it when He blocks their path. They would never choose to put it on their itinerary. But as they take the road out, they can be grateful that God put it on their itinerary. As they reflect on it, they may well join Robert Browning Hamilton in saying:

I walked a mile with pleasure, She chattered all the way;
But she left me none the wiser, For all she had to say.

I walked a mile with sorrow, Not one word said she;
But, oh, the things I learned, When sorrow walked with me.

Above, Near, Around, and Beneath

FROM GOD'S WORD, THE BIBLE...

There is no one like the God of Jeshurun,
Who rides the heavens to help you,
And in His excellency on the clouds.
The eternal God is your refuge,
And underneath are the everlasting arms;
He will thrust out the enemy from before you,
And will say, "Destroy!"

DEUTERONOMY 33:26-27

After leading the people of Israel for forty years, the time has come for Moses to say goodbye. In Deuteronomy 33 we have his farewell address. It falls into three easily discernible parts. There is an introductory statement (vv. 2-5), a blessing for the nation's individual tribes (vv. 6-25) and a closing blessing on the nation (vv. 26-29).

That closing blessing . . .what wonderful nuggets of truth it contains! How they must have cheered the hearts of the listening Israelites! Here they are: God is above you, near you, around you, and beneath you. Put them all together, and you have Moses saying this to Israel—God is totally sufficient for you.

God above them? Yes, here it is:

There is no one like the God of Jeshurun,
Who rides the heavens. . .

The name "Jeshurun," meaning "upright one," may have been an affectionate term for the nation of Israel. This much we know for sure—Moses wanted his people to understand that there was no one who could compare to their God. They were poised to enter the land of Canaan. There they would encounter many new gods, but their God was the true God and over all other gods.

God was also near them:

. . .Who rides the heavens to help you. . .

Does that mean God was near them? Sure, it does. One has to be near to help.

The Israelites had already experienced God's nearness—abundantly so! He drew near or came down (Ex. 2:8) to deliver their fathers from slavery in the land of Egypt. And He would be near to help this new generation as they faced the challenges ahead.

What about the truth that God was around them? Where do we find it? It's right here:

The eternal God is your refuge. . .

When the people of Israel entered the land of Canaan, they would find many refuges, that is, cities with high walls. The Canaanites were surrounded and protected by those walls. The Israelites, on the other hand, dwelled in flimsy tents. How could they, a tent-dwelling people, hope to conquer those mighty fortresses?

Moses assured them that God would be their refuge or fortress. He would surround and protect them as those imposing walls protected the Canaanites.

So we come to the final truth—God was beneath them. Moses says:

And underneath are the everlasting arms. . .

The challenges facing the people of Israel were so daunting that the Israelites would sometimes feel as if they were falling into failure. Moses assured them that God would be there to catch and lift them.

An ancient leader saying farewell to an ancient people! Is that all we have here? No, there is more, and the more is that the truths Moses put before Israel are just as much for us as they were for them.

God is *above* us. He is the same God now as He was then. He was not limited in wisdom and power in Moses' time, and He is not lim-ited today. He is ever the sovereign ruler of the universe who is greater than all the forces of evil.

God is *near* us. He is as near to us as He was to Israel of old. God drew near when He sent His Son and told Joseph to call Him "Im-manuel," which means "God with us." Our Immanuel is the one who has promised to be with us always (Matt. 28:20).

God is *around* us. He has surrounded us with the walls of salvation which protect us from eternal loss (Isa. 26:2). That salvation is found in the Lord Jesus Christ who bore on the cross the penalty for sin-ners so that all who trust in Him in His atoning death will never have to bear that penalty themselves.

God is *beneath* us. Christians will never be perfect in this life. Of-tentimes we fail. And Satan is eager to suggest that failure means that God will have nothing more to do with us. It is not true. No saint of God can ever fall so far that the arms of God are not there to catch and lift him or her.

March 3

Four Men, Two Worlds

FROM GOD'S WORD, THE BIBLE...

So he answered, "Do not fear, for those who are with us are more than those who are with them." And Elisha prayed, and said, "LORD, I pray, open his eyes that he may see." Then the LORD opened the eyes of the young man, and he saw. And behold, the mountain was full of horses and chariots of fire all around Elisha.

FROM 2 KINGS 6:8-17
(Read 2 Kings 6 for this meditation.)

There are four men in this passage of Scripture, and I think I must be here as well. The king of Syria is here. He was one who had no regard for the one and only true God. The king of Israel is also here. He was a man who professed faith in the living God but actually lived in defiance of Him. The prophet Elisha is here. He was a man of towering faith who lived in close communion with the Lord.

I certainly hope I am not either of these two kings. I know I am not the prophet Elisha—not on my very best day. I think I must be the fourth man in this passage—the servant of Elisha. He is the man who cried out to his master: "Alas . . . what shall we do?" I wonder if you find yourself in this man? But let's back up a little.

The king of Syria was all aflutter. He was trying to wage war on the king of Israel, but it wasn't going well. Someone was telling Israel's king every move that he, the king of Syria, was about to make. Thinking he had a traitor among his servants, he called them together. It was then that he discovered his problem. One of his servants let the cat out of the bag: ". . .Elisha, the prophet who is in Israel, tells the king of Israel the words that you speak in your bedroom" (v. 12).

So the king of Syria decided to send a "great army" to Dothan, where Elisha was, to take him into custody.

It was nighttime when the army arrived and surrounded the city. When Elisha's servant arose and peered through the early morning gloom, he saw the army. There were Syrian soldiers everywhere! That's when he said to Elisha: "Alas, my master! What shall we do?" (v. 15).

Elisha was ready with the answer: "Do not fear, for those who are with us are more than those who are with them" (v. 16). Then Elisha asked the Lord to open his servant's eyes, and the servant saw "horses and chariots of fire all around Elisha" (v. 17).

As I look at our world, it sometimes seems as if there is nothing to see but "Syrians." The enemies of God are so numerous, so powerful, and so ferocious that it often seems that there is no hope, and we tremble for the future of the kingdom of God. It is easy to give in to fear of evil and evil times. There are always plenty of Syrians to see! This passage tells us to overcome our fear of the forces of evil by looking beyond them to the invisible forces of heaven.

We sorely need this passage. It reminds us that this world—the visible world—is not all that there is. There is another world. It is the world of God and the angels. It is the spiritual and eternal world. It is far greater than this world that we can see. It is always aware of what is going on in this world and can at any time break in for the glory of God and the good of God's people.

For a long time Nebuchadnezzar could see nothing but his glorious kingdom of Babylon. But God showed him that there was a far greater kingdom than Babylon and a far greater king than himself (Dan. 4:17). His grandson, Belshazzar, also loved the world that he could see, but then a hand appeared from the world that he could not see and wrote a message that caused him to tremble (Dan. 5).

The key to living in this world is to keep looking by faith at the unseen world. It is to endure as Moses did by "seeing Him who is invisible" (Heb. 11:27).

That unseen world will not always be unseen. We will all have to enter it someday, and the only way to enter it safely is through faith in the Lord Jesus Christ. By the way, He, Jesus, is the greatest evidence of the reality of that world. He came from it and steadily revealed the existence of it in His words, His miracles, His death on the cross, and His resurrection.

Three Gifts from a Queen

From God's Word, the Bible...

So Mordecai went out from the presence of the king in royal apparel of blue and white, with a great crown of gold and a garment of fine linen and purple; and the city of Shushan rejoiced and was glad. The Jews had light and gladness, joy and honor. And in every province and city, wherever the king's command and decree came, the Jews had joy and gladness, a feast and a holiday. Then many of the people of the land became Jews, because fear of the Jews fell upon them.

Esther 8:15-17

The queen I have in mind is Esther, a beautiful Jewish woman who, through a very unlikely chain of events, rose from obscurity to become queen of Persia at some point in the time span of 485-464 B.C.

The book of Esther tells us of her heroism during a time of crisis. When we read this book, which is one of only two in the Bible that bears the name of a woman, it is as if Esther herself were standing before us and extending her hands to offer three gifts.

The first is *the gift of realism*. The book of Esther reminds us of the ongoing reality of evil in this world, evil which is often expressed in the persecution of God's people.

We can't go very far into this book before we meet one of the most unsavory, despicable human beings to ever occupy the human stage. His name? Haman!

This man was appointed by King Ahasuerus of Persia to serve as his prime minister. He, Haman, would be second only to the king himself in terms of power and authority.

Here we have a glaring example of the terrible results of putting bad people into high offices.

The mistake of appointing the vile Haman was bad enough, but the king made it worse by commanding all the citizens to bow when Haman walked by. One man refused to comply—a Jew named Mordecai. Here now is the vileness of Haman: because Mordecai refused to bow before him, Haman hatched a plot to have Mordecai and all the Jews of Persia executed. He went to the king to have this plot approved, and the king, making yet another horrible mistake, granted Haman's request.

What reason did Haman give for wanting the Jews exterminated? They were different (Est. 3:8).

Persecution of Christians is growing exponentially around the world. The reason? Oftentimes, it is that they, by virtue of their convictions, cannot go along with political correctness. They're different.

The book of Esther doesn't sugarcoat things. It tells us to expect to encounter the evils of hatred and persecution. It tells us to be realistic.

A second gift from Esther is *the gift of assurance.*

One of the unusual things about this book is that it doesn't mention God. But while His name isn't here, He is here. He is here to overrule evil and to care for His people. In troubling and threatening times, we need nothing more than this calm assurance: God is at work even when He seems not to be, and the work He is doing is for the glory of His name and the good of His people.

Undiscerning people will read Esther and marvel at the sequence of unlikely events. They will call them "coincidences." They are actually "providences," that is, God guiding events to accomplish His purposes. It was the guiding hand of God that brought Esther to the throne, that brought about the execution of the hateful Haman, and that delivered the Jews.

But the best gift Esther gives us is *the gift of Christ.* Christ in the book of Esther? Absolutely!

What we have in this book is God working through a mediator (Esther) to save His people from the sentence of death.

A mediator is a go-between. To save her people, Esther stepped between the one who had issued the death decree (the king) and her people. She pleaded with the king on behalf of her people, and the king issued another decree that effectively spared the Jews.

The Lord Jesus is the mediator between God and sinners. God has handed down the sentence of eternal destruction on all of us as the just penalty for our sins. But Jesus stepped between us and that decree. He received the wrath that decree demands so all who believe in Him will never have to endure that wrath themselves.

So the greatest gift of the book of Esther is that it points us to One greater than Esther. While we thank God for her, we thank Him even more for Jesus.

Which Bird Should I Be?

From God's Word, the Bible...

I am like a pelican of the wilderness;
I am like an owl of the desert.
I lie awake,
And am like a sparrow alone on the housetop.

Psalm 102:6-7

How often David must have been a bird-watcher! In Psalm 55:6, he mentions the dove, and in Psalm 102:6-7, the pelican, the owl, and the sparrow. (It's true that Psalm 102 does not identify him as its author, but it seems very much in the style of David.)

The pelican, owl, and sparrow represented David as he sometimes found himself to be. These birds are fitting emblems for loneliness. The pelican is away from his natural habitat and alone in the wilderness. The owl is alone in the desert. The sparrow sits alone on the housetop.

The pelican and the owl are also known for their soft moaning.

David could easily identify with those birds. He was so burdened and troubled that he felt all alone and went along softly moaning. And we have no trouble identifying with David. We know what it is to have what we might describe as the pelican problem. We sometimes feel utterly alone and helpless. Our hearts are so heavy that we moan as we go along. Our experience and burdens are such that the wilderness seems to be a fitting image for the world in which we live.

What was causing David to feel so burdened? It was the problem he so often expresses in the Psalms—his enemies. He writes in Psalm 102:8:

My enemies reproach me all day long;
And those who deride me swear an oath against me.

In Psalm 55, we find another instance of David moaning (v. 2) for the same reason—the hatred of his enemies (v. 3). On this occasion, he thought of another bird—the gentle, peaceful dove. That dove represented David as he often wished he could be. He writes yearningly in verse 6:

Oh, that I had wings like a dove!
For then I would fly away and be at rest...

Have you ever wished you could just fly away and "be at rest"? How often in these stress-filled times we hear someone say: "I need to get away from it for a while!" As we increasingly face the Christophobia of this time—the resistance to biblical Christianity—we might find ourselves longing to escape and find peace. Or it may simply be our personal pressures and responsibilities that make us feel that way.

There is yet another bird that represents David as he knew he should always be. While David doesn't specifically name that bird, we have no trouble identifying it. We are now in Psalm 57, and David's problem has once again raised its ugly head. There are people who would "swallow" him up (v. 3), individuals who were more like lions than people. They were ready to devour him (v. 4) and to entrap him (v.6).

So what bird came to David's mind on this occasion? It was not the dove. It was the little chick. David says to the Lord (v. 1):

And in the shadow of Your wings I will make my refuge,
Until these calamities have passed by.

When danger arises, the mother hen clucks and spreads her wings, and the little chicks immediately run under those wings and stay there until the danger has passed.

We might say David has traded wings! He has traded the wings of the dove for the wings of the mother hen. He realized that he didn't need *escaping* wings because he had in the Lord *sheltering* wings.

How do we run to God and find shelter? We must run to His Word. There is a "clucking" there. God warns us of danger and extends comfort to us in His Word, but it will be of no avail to us if we do not avail ourselves of it.

Then we must run to prayer. David writes (v. 2):

I will cry out to God Most High,
To God who performs all things for me.

And we run to God by running to praise, saying with David (vv. 7, 11):

I will sing and give praise.
. . .Be exalted, O God, above the heavens;
Let Your glory be above all the earth.

Which bird should I be? I, and you, should be like the little chick. When we feel like a pelican, we should not act like a dove; rather, we should learn to act like a chick taking refuge in the everlasting shelter of the wings of the Almighty.

The Worst Kind of Forgetfulness

From God's Word, the Bible...

In those days Hezekiah was sick and near death, and he prayed to the Lord; and He spoke to him and gave him a sign. But Hezekiah did not repay according to the favor shown him, for his heart was lifted up; therefore wrath was looming over him and over Judah and Jerusalem. Then Hezekiah humbled himself for the pride of his heart, he and the inhabitants of Jerusalem, so that the wrath of the Lord did not come upon them in the days of Hezekiah.

2 Chronicles 32:24-26

Most of us wage an ongoing battle with forgetfulness. We find ourselves forgetting appointments, names, and faces. Most episodes of our forgetfulness are annoying but harmless. We forget where we put our keys and we are delayed for a few minutes. But no real damage is done. There are times, however, when forgetfulness can be very harmful indeed.

Meet Hezekiah, king of Judah. Here is a man who fell into the worst kind of forgetfulness, and it was anything but harmless. Here is a man who forgot to be grateful.

If there was ever a man who had lots of reasons to be thankful, it was Hezekiah. He and his kingdom had been delivered from the threat of being conquered by Sennacherib, the powerful king of Assyria (v. 22). In addition to that, the Lord had given Hezekiah prominence in the eyes of the surrounding nations (v. 23). Then there was that episode in which the Lord graciously promised to extend Hezekiah's life by fifteen years (Isa. 38:5).

These are only three of the many, many blessings the Lord bestowed on Hezekiah. He was an abundantly blessed man, and, as such, he should have been abundantly thankful. And we expect to read that he was, but, shockingly enough, we read: "Hezekiah did not repay according to the favor shown him. . ." (v. 25).

There is no way anyone can ever repay God for blessings, but one can at the very least demonstrate his or her gratitude by truly worshiping Him (Heb. 13:15) and by obeying His commandments (Luke 6:46).

Hezekiah failed. Although he had been so signally blessed by God, he turned his back on Him. Why did he do it? His heart was "lifted up" with pride (v. 25).

There are plenty of thanksgiving-killers—being busy with responsibilities and pleasures, being occupied with the problems of life, failing to walk in close communion with the Lord. But there is no more prolific thanksgiving-killer than pride. Pride kills thanksgiving because it causes us to think we deserve what we receive. We are not grateful for things we deserve. They are owed to us, and it is only right and fair that we should have them.

We are grateful, however, for those things that are given to us without our deserving them. And here is the thing we so often lose sight of—we don't really deserve anything at all. Everything we have is given to us, not because we deserve it, but rather because of the goodness and grace of God.

Hezekiah emerges from the pages of Scripture as a reminder to be careful about thanksgiving. Every child of God can and should join the psalmist in saying:

Blessed be the LORD,
Who daily loads us with benefits,
The God of our salvation.
(Ps. 68:19)

God has, as it were, loaded the wagons of our lives with the bounty of heaven. What do we consider to be good? Family? Health? Friends? Material wellbeing? All come from God (James 1:17).

In addition to these things, the children of God have received the most wonderful blessing the Lord has to bestow—forgiveness for sin and eternal life through the redeeming work of Jesus.

Who can calculate the greatness of this? The Second Person of the Trinity, who was fully God, left the glories of heaven and came to this earth in our humanity. He rendered perfect obedience to God, thus providing for sinners the righteousness they need to stand acceptably before God. Then He went to the cross to actually receive the wrath of God, thus paying the penalty our sins deserve. Christianity in a nutshell is this—He got our sins and we get His righteousness (2 Cor. 5:21).

What a blessing! And all are invited to come and receive what Christ has done.

If we have received it, gratitude should reign in our lives. We must not forget what God has done for us in Christ. No Christian can forget forever, but to even forget for a while is the worst kind of forgetfulness.

March 7

Reminders from Molly

From God's Word, the Bible...

Offer to God thanksgiving,
And pay your vows to the Most High.

Psalm 50:1

...bearing with one another, and forgiving one another, if anyone has a complaint against another; even as Christ forgave you, so you also must do.

Colossians 3:13

The Bible tells us to consider the ant (Prov. 6:6) and to look at the birds (Matt. 6:26). It points us to the ox and the donkey (Isa. 1:3) and also to the deer (Ps. 42:1). So it is obvious that animals can teach us vital and valuable lessons.

My wife and I have a dog named Molly. Molly is a Morkie: half Maltese, half Yorkie.

Molly has many qualities that I admire, and a few, well, not so much.

One of Molly's admirable traits is gratitude.

Every time we eat a meal, I feed Molly a few morsels. After the meal is over, I usually sit in my easy chair. Invariably, Molly jumps on my lap and begins to lick my face and wag her tail. I'm sure it's her way of expressing gratitude to me for sharing my food with her.

I learned as a child the importance of gratitude, but I need to be reminded. Molly reminds me. I think she knows that I will continue to take care of her even if she doesn't express gratitude. But she can't help herself. Gratitude is so much a part of her nature that she has to express it. She is rich in gratitude.

We need to work hard to make sure we are grateful for God's greatest blessing—salvation through His Son, the Lord Jesus. That should daily fill our hearts and call forth our praise. But being thankful for that blessing does not fully discharge our responsibility. We are to be thankful for all of God's blessings. Paul urges us to be "...giving thanks always for all things to God the Father in the name of our Lord Jesus Christ..." (Eph. 5:20). In 1 Thessalonians 5:18, he adds: "...in everything give thanks, for this is the will of God in Christ Jesus for you."

"For" and "in" are little words with large meaning! Be thankful for all things and in all things.

Let's get back to Molly. She also reminds me that failure doesn't have to be final. A good bit of each day for Molly is sitting on our back porch watching for squirrels to come into our fenced yard. They do come often to eat the seeds that fall to the ground from our bird feeder. When a squirrel arrives, Molly immediately goes into her stalking mode. Inching forward ever so slightly, she imagines each time that she will finally catch the elusive squirrel. She never does. But that doesn't keep her from trying. She refuses to accept failure as final.

We fail in our Christian walk many times, and the devil is ever anxious to assure us that our failures are so severe that the Lord wants nothing more to do with us. But failure is not final for the Christian. Simon Peter failed miserably when he denied the Lord three times, but the Lord was not through with him. When we fail, we must not lie down in our failure but ask the Lord to forgive us and start moving forward again.

Molly also reminds me to be a quick-forgiver. Molly does not have a doghouse, but she sometimes gets in the doghouse, if you know what I mean. Although she has to be rebuked and corrected, she doesn't hold it against my wife or me. And she doesn't hold it against us when we take her to the veterinarian. She forgets and forgives quickly.

The Bible calls all believers not to nurse resentment and bitterness but to forgive. Paul writes: "And be kind to one another, tenderhearted, forgiving one another, just as God in Christ also forgave you" (Eph. 4:32).

Most of all Molly reminds me of the importance of love and trust. She loves us unconditionally and she trusts us to do what is good and right for her. Every Christian loves the Lord, and every Christian trusts the Lord. But love and trust are always matters of degree. They do not always stay the same. They fluctuate and vacillate. Molly's love for me and trust in me seem to be unchanging. They are always at the same high level.

I need to be more like Molly.

March 8

Mr. Debatable

From God's Word, the Bible...

So Elijah went to present himself to Ahab; and there was a severe famine in Samaria. And Ahab had called Obadiah, who was in charge of his house. (Now Obadiah feared the Lord greatly. For so it was, while Jezebel massacred the prophets of the Lord, that Obadiah had taken one hundred prophets and hidden them, fifty to a cave, and had fed them with bread and water.) And Ahab had said to Obadiah, "Go into the land to all the springs of water and to all the brooks; perhaps we may find grass to keep the horses and mules alive, so that we will not have to kill any livestock." So they divided the land between them to explore it; Ahab went one way by himself, and Obadiah went another way by himself.

From 1 Kings 18:1-16

Who is Mr. Debatable? It is none other than Obadiah, the servant of the extremely vile and wicked King Ahab.

I call him Mr. Debatable because students of the Bible are divided on whether he is a man to be commended or one to be condemned. I lean toward the former. My summary of Obadiah goes like this: in tough times he was a good man who had moments of weakness.

Tough times? Without a doubt! It was the time when Ahab and Jezebel ruled the nation of Israel.

A little bit now about Jezebel; she was a Sidonian who came into her marriage to Ahab with a radical commitment to the god Baal. Baal was a nature god. He supposedly controlled the weather and thus secured for his devotees the fertility of the land and an abundant harvest.

Her husband, Ahab, may very well have been more of a syncretist or synthesist, that is, he may have thought that he could synthesize or blend the worship of Baal with the worship of God. Jezebel was no synthesist. She was all out for Baal. It was Baal or nothing in her book.

We may find it hard to believe, but Baal worship by this time had grown so much that it had almost taken over Israel. A nation so immensely blessed by God had now set God aside.

This was also the time of the prophet Elijah. He is the one who came storming into Ahab's presence to announce that there would be no rain in Israel until he, Elijah, said so.

Three-and-a-half years passed, and there had not been a drop of rain. So much for Baal controlling the weather!

Now back to Mr. Debatable! During those exceedingly difficult times, Obadiah performed admirably. Jezebel was out to kill every prophet of the Lord, but Obadiah, at the risk of losing his life, hid one hundred of them and sustained them with food and water. Where did he get the water in this time of drought? We do not know.

If Obadiah performed so heroically, what is so debatable about him? It's because he had some moments of weakness when Elijah suddenly showed up and asked him to arrange a meeting with Ahab. Obadiah began to waver. He feared for his life. He thought he would get the meeting arranged, Elijah would again disappear, and he, Obadiah, would be executed on the spot. Obadiah wavered when the chips were down, much like Simon Peter would do centuries later when he denied the Lord Jesus three times.

But Obadiah's wavering was temporary. The Word of the Lord was confronting him through Elijah. Obadiah initially preferred that the Word work apart from his own involvement, and he had no trouble coming up with an excuse. But the Word continued to press upon him until it won his heart. The Word pressed and pressed until it overcame his reluctance and halfheartedness and propelled him into obedience. So we read these blessed words: "So Obadiah went to meet Ahab, and told him; and Ahab went to meet Elijah" (v. 16).

Let's picture Elijah as the representative of the Word of God and Obadiah as the representative of the people of God. In Elijah's command to Obadiah to go to Ahab, we have God's Word taking hold of God's people and pressing them into service.

God's Word still does that. It still speaks to God's people. We can so easily be like Obadiah. We can desire for the Word to do its work while we sit on the sidelines and cheer. It's so very easy for us to want the Lord to address the Ahabs of this world without addressing us.

We need revival. In times of revival, the first thing the Lord does is address His own people (2 Chron. 7:14). He calls upon them to repudiate and renounce their halfheartedness and their desire for private discipleship so that they can be channels for His holy Word.

Was Obadiah's performance debatable? No more than the performance of God's people today! Isn't it good to know that the God who did not give up on him does not give up on us?

March 9

Does the Devil Go to Church?

FROM GOD'S WORD, THE BIBLE...

For such are false apostles, deceitful workers, transforming themselves into apostles of Christ. And no wonder! For Satan himself transforms himself into an angel of light. Therefore it is no great thing if his ministers also transform themselves into ministers of righteousness, whose end will be according to their works.

2 CORINTHIANS 11:13-15
(Also read Mark 4:1-20 for this meditation.)

Let's not be in doubt about the existence of the devil. He is a real person. He started out as one of God's angels, perhaps even the greatest among the angels. But he became full of himself and actually thought that he could be God. So he persuaded other angels to join him in an attempt to defeat and dethrone God. But it didn't work—rebellion against God never does—and he and his angels were cast out of heaven. So Lucifer ("morning star" or, more literally, "son of the morning")—that was his original name—became Satan. The name Satan means "adversary." As the name suggests, Satan's grand scheme is to oppose God.

Let's turn our attention to the church of the Lord Jesus. There is so very much that we could say about her, but at this point we should focus on one thing in particular—the church's special connection to the truth of God. The Apostle Paul calls her "the pillar and ground of the truth" (1 Tim. 3:15). As pillars and foundations hold up or support a building, so the church is to uphold and support the truth of God's Word and, more particularly, the truth of the gospel.

The church is to love, support, and exalt the truth of God. She is to rejoice when the truth is held high, and mourn when the truth is cast down into the mire.

The devil hates the truth of God with the utmost hatred. He labors to undermine, defeat, and destroy it.

Now to our question—does the devil go to church? That depends. There is no need for him to attend churches that have no interest in God's truth. There is no work for him to do in such churches. The work is already done. Such churches are not really churches. They have the name, but that is all.

There are churches that the devil loves to attend—Bible-believing, Bible-preaching churches in which Christ is exalted. It is hard to get people to attend such churches, but Satan never misses a service.

It would seem that the devil would stay away from such services. Why would he expose himself to the truth that he so hates? J.C. Ryle writes of Satan:

. . .nowhere perhaps is the devil so active as in a congregation of Gospel-hearers. . . . From him come wandering thoughts and roving imaginations,–listless minds and dull memories,—sleepy eyes and fidgety nerves,—weary ears and distracted attention. . . .We shall always find him at Church. He never stays away from public ordinances. Let us remember this, and be upon our guard.[4]

If we think this sounds fanciful and far-fetched, we need to revisit Jesus' parable of the sower. The sower goes out to his field to sow his seed. The seed would be God's Word, and the sower the preacher. As the sower sows, the seed falls on various types of ground—"wayside" ground, stony ground, thorny ground, and good ground. These represent the hearers. Of the "wayside" hearers, Jesus says: "And when they hear, Satan comes immediately and takes away the word that was sown in their hearts" (Mark 4:15).

Amazingly enough, Satan may even attend church as the preacher. The Apostle Paul says: ". . .Satan himself transforms himself into an angel of light. Therefore it is no great thing if his ministers also transform themselves into ministers of righteousness, whose end will be according to their works" (2 Cor. 11:14-15).

Satan at church! In the pulpit and in the pew! What a sobering thought! Let's make sure we keep our wits about us even while we are in church, and let's seek to love and support the truth as much as Satan hates and opposes it.

4 *Expository Thoughts on Luke, vol. i,* The Banner of Truth Trust, Edinburgh, 1986, pp. 250-1

The Worm Crushing the Mountain

FROM GOD'S WORD, THE BIBLE...

"Fear not, you worm Jacob,
You men of Israel!
I will help you," says the LORD
And your Redeemer, the Holy One of Israel.
"Behold, I will make you into a new threshing sledge with sharp teeth;
You shall thresh the mountains and beat them small,
And make the hills like chaff.
You shall winnow them, the wind shall carry them away,
And the whirlwind shall scatter them;
You shall rejoice in the LORD,
And glory in the Holy One of Israel."

ISAIAH 41:14-16

Worms are lowly, helpless little creatures, and mountains are majestic and mighty. What we have in these verses, then, is the promise that the lowly and helpless will destroy the mighty and majestic.

We could easily dismiss this as lunacy if it were not for the fact that it was the Lord who promised this, and it has already come true.

The worm in this passage refers to God's people. The Lord says:

Fear not, you worm, Jacob,
You men of Israel!

The mountains refer to the difficulties facing God's people at that time. It was a most challenging and serious time. The people of God had seemingly lost everything. Their homes and cities lay in ruins, their temple was demolished, and they themselves were captives in distant Babylon.

Babylon was so very powerful, and the Jews so very weak. If we had been there to observe and to give odds on the Jews returning home from Babylon, we might have said: "It would be about the same odds as a worm crushing a mountain!"

But that worm did crush that mountain. Babylon was defeated, and the Jews returned home. It was not because the weak Jews suddenly became powerful. It was all God's doing. The Lord had promised to help them (v. 14), and help them He did. He raised up the Persians to defeat Babylon, and He put it into the heart of the Persian king, Cyrus, to release the Jews.

The church today seems very much like a worm in the face of an increasingly anti-Christian world. Where is her hope? It's in the Lord who can cause worms to level mountains. He has helped His church in the past, and He still has the ability to help her today. He has promised that the gates of hell will not prevail against her (Matt. 16:18).

There is also encouragement in this passage for individual believers who are facing hardships. Our God is a helping God! He may not help us as quickly as we would like. (The Jews were in captivity for seventy years before they were released.) And He may not help us in the ways that we would like. But we must never doubt that God helps His people.

Believers were once facing the largest of all difficulties. We were in our sins and under the righteous condemnation of God. We were part of Satan's domain and facing the wrath of God. We had no more chance of overcoming these difficulties than a worm has of crushing a mountain.

But our helping God stepped in! He who identifies Himself as the "Redeemer" (v. 14) has redeemed us. He has taken us out of our sins and given us eternal life.

How did God accomplish this for us? The answer is written large in Scripture. It was through His Son, the Lord Jesus Christ. More specifically, it was through His Son going to the cross to die in our stead. On that cross, Jesus received the wrath of God so all who believe in Him would never have to receive that wrath themselves.

We find in Psalm 22 a detailed anticipation of Jesus' death on the cross. It is essentially the Lord Jesus Himself describing His death centuries before it occurred. At one point, He cries:

But I am a worm, and no man;
A reproach of men, and despised of the people.
(Ps. 22:6)

Our ability to deal with our sins was on a par with the ability of a worm to crush a mountain, but Jesus became a worm in our stead and crushed for us the mountain of condemnation.

When our circumstances are harsh, let's remember that God has already helped us by doing for us the greatest thing He could do. He has provided salvation for us. If God has already helped us in that way, we may rest assured that He will help us in every other situation.

The redeeming work of God will one day culminate in His people leaving this realm of tears and coming into eternal glory. We will most certainly be amazed that we are there, and we will be keenly aware that we do not deserve to be there. And when we hear one of our fellow-saints say: "Isn't this amazing?" we may be inclined to answer: "Yes, it's like worms crushing mountains."

Look to the Hippo

From God's Word, the Bible...

Look now at the behemoth,which I made along with you;
He eats grass like an ox.

Job 40:15

Job was deeply devoted to the Lord. He was also a very prosperous man. One day Satan came before the Lord to discuss Job. Satan suggested that Job was faithful to God because He had so abundantly blessed him. If the Lord were to withdraw His blessings, Satan argued, Job would immediately turn against Him.

The Lord took up the challenge. He gave Satan permission to remove Job's prosperity, and remove it Satan did. When he was through, Job was without children, herds, herdsmen, and health. All he had left was his wife and some friends, all of whom insisted on giving him bad advice.

Most of the book is taken up with that bad advice and with Job's response to it. The book comes to a close with the Lord Himself speaking to Job (38:1-41:34). God never tells Job about Satan's challenge and His response. He primarily asks Job a series of questions that are designed to point out His greatness. In the midst of these questions, the Lord tells Job to look at the "behemoth." This is a reference to a beast of some kind. Many commentators think it is the hippopotamus or even a dinosaur.

What an amazing thing! Job was suffering horribly, and yet God tells him to look at the hippo. This seems to be the totally inadequate answer of the adequate God.

Can you relate to this? Do you sometimes feel that God is giving you totally inadequate answers to the challenges and crises of life? Perhaps you are facing harsh difficulties, and when you look to God it seems as if He is telling you to look to the hippo!

We can be sure that God has the answers we need. There is nothing going on in our lives that He cannot explain. He knows why you or your family member is sick; He knows why your loved one died; He knows why this world is such a mess. You cannot possibly ask God a question that He cannot answer.

But the fact that God knows the answers doesn't mean that He shares them with us. God has often puzzled His people by doing things that didn't seem to make sense.

Here, then, is the question: why would God tell Job to look at a great creature such as a hippopotamus? The answer would seem to be that it takes more wisdom and power to make a hippopotamus than we realize. The Lord intended that Job would draw this conclusion: if God had enough wisdom and power to make a hippo, He had enough wisdom and power to govern Job's life.

Job's responsibility in the midst of his searing adversity was not to question God but rather to bow before His wisdom and power. And God's call to Job is His call to us. When the circumstances of life seem to be too difficult for us, we must always remember that there is a divine wisdom at work in our circumstances.

Here now is a man hanging on a Roman cross outside Jerusalem, and God points to that cross and tells us that the only way our sins can be forgiven is through that man hanging on that cross. He tells us that man is not dying there as other men died on other crosses. He died a special kind of death. He actually received an eternity's worth of the wrath of God in the place of sinners. If we want to be delivered from that wrath, we must repent of our sins and accept from our hearts what that man did on that cross.

A man dying on a cross 2,000 years ago is the way of salvation? It seems so inadequate. Laden down with the guilt of our sins, we come to God, and He points us to that cross. It seems as if He is mocking us. We have this horrible problem, and He tells us to look to the hippo! But God's wisdom and power are in that cross (1 Cor. 1:18-25), and if we are to be saved we must bow before it.

Look to the hippo; and, once you have looked to the hippo, look beyond and up to the man God appointed—the man Christ Jesus—whose saving work on the cross is sufficient for needy sinners such as we all are.

March 12

Searching Questions from a Miserable Man

FROM GOD'S WORD, THE BIBLE...

Will the Lord cast off forever?
And will He be favorable no more?
Has His mercy ceased forever?
Has His promise failed forevermore?
Has God forgotten to be gracious?
Has He in anger shut up His tender mercies? Selah
And I said, "This is my anguish;
But I will remember the years of the right hand of the Most High."
I will remember the works of the LORD;
Surely I will remember Your wonders of old.
I will also meditate on all Your work,
And talk of Your deeds.

PSALM 77:7-12

What was it anyway? What was causing Asaph, the author of this psalm, to be so miserable?

He was miserable. There can be no doubt about that. In verse 2 he mentions the day of his trouble. In the same verse he says this trouble was so deep and serious that his soul refused to be comforted.

In verse 3 he tells us that even the thought of God did not bring him any comfort. He also indicates that his spirit was overwhelmed. In verse 4, he says he couldn't sleep. He also tells us that he couldn't even talk about his trouble. Most of us find relief by being able to share our troubles with our friends, but not Asaph.

Had he wrecked his new chariot? Was he facing an audit from the tax authorities? Had his favorite team lost an important game?

Are you ready for this? Asaph tells us that his misery came from considering the past:

I have considered the days of old,
The years of ancient times. (v. 5)

Why did he find the past to be so troubling? Was there some great, glaring failure there that now raised its ugly head to fill him with regret and guilt? Not at all! The past he was considering was good. It was one in which he had a song in the night (v. 6).

Why would a good past vex him and make him so miserable? It made him realize that his present couldn't begin to compare to that wonderful past. Asaph was in trouble because he could look at the past and see marvelous instances of God at work in his life and in the lives of those around him. But the present was such that there were no such instances or evidences of God at work.

As you view your present situation, maybe like Asaph you feel in your experience and circumstances as if

- God has cast you off forever and God has decided to be favorable to you no more (see v. 7)
- God's mercy has ceased forever and God's promise has failed (see v. 8)
- God has forgotten to be gracious and God in anger has locked up all His tender mercies and thrown away the key (see v. 9).

Asaph was in a terrible state because the people of God had enjoyed a glorious past? Really? That seems bizarre, but that is exactly what Asaph tells us. He says:

This is my anguish.(v. 10)

Anguish is not the final word for Asaph. There in verse 10 he also turns the corner. As he reflected on the glories of the past, he suddenly realized that he had been looking at them in the wrong way. Instead of letting those glories depress him, he should have been letting them bless him. The fact that God had worked so mightily in the past meant that there was hope for the future. The God of the past hasn't changed. He is still the same, and, no matter how bleak and dreary our circumstances are, they are not greater than our God. He can break in and do glorious things today even as He did in bygone days.

Asaph's account of his bout with despondency forces us to ask ourselves some very penetrating and searching questions:

- Are we as concerned about the current condition of the people of God as Asaph was? If not, why not? There is certainly plenty to be concerned about.
- What are we doing about the current situation? Are we crying to God regarding it? Are we seeking His face, or have we fallen into the trap of merely lamenting the situation?
- Are we assuming that it is impossible for us to see a mighty moving of God's Spirit, that such a moving is a thing of the past and cannot be repeated? Do we think that the times in which we live are too hard for God? Or are we letting the fact that God has moved powerfully in the past to encourage us to believe that He can move powerfully again?

May the experience of Asaph encourage us to lay hold of God in prayer—and as a result, may we live well for Him in the grace of the gospel of the Lord Jesus Christ.

Should You Growl Like a Bear?

FROM GOD'S WORD, THE BIBLE...

No one calls for justice,
Nor does any plead for truth.
They trust in empty words and speak lies;
They conceive evil and bring forth iniquity.
They hatch vipers' eggs and weave the spider's web;
He who eats of their eggs dies,
And from that which is crushed a viper breaks out.

We all growl like bears,
And moan sadly like doves;
We look for justice, but there is none;
For salvation, but it is far from us.

ISAIAH 59:4-5, 11
See also Isaiah 59:20.

One day the Spirit of God tapped the prophet Isaiah on the shoulder and said: "I want you to hear something." So the prophet leaned over, put his ear on the windowpane of the future and listened intently. And what did he hear? Growling and moaning! More precisely, he heard the growling of bears and the moaning of doves. The growling was the sound of angry complaining, while the moaning was the sound of sadness.

Where would all this growling and moaning come from? It would come from Isaiah's people, the people of Judah. And when would it occur? Several years after Isaiah died! What would cause it? Their captivity in Babylon!

Bears growl when they are impatient for food, and there in Babylon the people would be impatient with God. They did, after all, consider themselves to be the people of God. Shouldn't that have translated into blessing instead of adversity? Do people who profess faith in God not have the right to expect His protection and care? But Isaiah's people would be experiencing problems, and there would seem to be no end in sight.

Would the people of Judah have a right to growl and moan in their time of captivity? Would they have reason to complain about God?

As Isaiah drew away from the windowpane of the future, the Spirit of God said to him: "I want you to write down the truth of the matter now. When the people begin to growl and moan in their captivity, they will be able to read what you write and the record will be set straight."

What did the Spirit want Isaiah to write? It was not a message that the people of Judah would want to hear, but it did set the record straight. The reason the people would be growling like bears in Babylon is because of their hatching of vipers' eggs and their weaving of spiders' webs (v. 5).

In other words, the people of Judah would have no reason to complain against God in their captivity because they themselves would be responsible for it. Their captivity would come about because of their nurturing of things that they should have destroyed.

If you were to find vipers' eggs in your backyard, what would you do? You certainly wouldn't hatch them and cuddle the vipers. You would destroy those eggs before the vipers hatched to destroy you.

For years and years, the people of Judah had nurtured things they should have destroyed. They had nurtured idolatry and immorality. God sent them prophet after prophet to urge them to destroy those things, but they refused to listen. When they finally ended up in captivity, they had no one to blame but themselves. To change the figure, they had woven for themselves a spider's web, and the captivity would be nothing more than them being trapped in the very web that they had woven.

The sad truth is that even in their captivity they continued for some time to cuddle their vipers before finally coming to their senses and turning back to God.

What about us? Are we nurturing things that will destroy us if we don't destroy them?

The Lord is ever kind to His people—even when He seems not to be kind. So the Spirit of God prompted Isaiah to include a marvelous note of hope. We might say the Spirit refused to leave them growling like bears.

Yes, the captivity would come about because of their bad choices, and, yes, it would be a difficult time. It would often seem to them as if God had totally abandoned them. But there was no cause for despair. God would come to them if they would sincerely turn from their sins in true repentance:

"The Redeemer will come to Zion,
And to those who turn from transgression in Jacob,"
Says the LORD.
(ISA. 59: 20)

What a marvelous message the Bible contains! It tells us that God can and does forgive those who have been so foolish as to hatch vipers' eggs. He can and does forgive on the basis of what Jesus did. He is the Redeemer promised in the above verse. The question is not whether God can forgive. It is, rather, whether we will repent.

Where to Turn in Times of Trouble

FROM GOD'S WORD, THE BIBLE...

For thus says the LORD: After seventy years are completed at Babylon, I will visit you and perform My good word toward you, and cause you to return to this place. For I know the thoughts that I think toward you, says the LORD, thoughts of peace and not of evil, to give you a future and a hope. Then you will call upon Me and go and pray to Me, and I will listen to you. And you will seek Me and find Me, when you search for Me with all your heart.

JEREMIAH 29:10-13

In 597 BC the Babylonians invaded the land of Judah and carried 3,023 citizens into captivity. This group included King Jehoiachin, his household, and some priests and prophets. The same Babylonians would return eleven years later and completely destroy Jerusalem and take practically all the remaining inhabitants into captivity.

After the initial captivity in 597 BC, word reached Jeremiah that some of the prophets who had been taken were predicting that Babylon would collapse soon and that there would be a speedy release for the captives.

When Jeremiah heard this, he wrote a letter to tell the captives that the captivity would last for at least seventy years (v. 10).

Jeremiah's letter must have come as a crushing blow for them. Their hope for a quick return wasn't to be. So what was left? Jeremiah's letter also gave them the answer to that question. He told them where to take refuge in those troubled times. Because we have troubles of our own, Jeremiah's answers are valid for us as well.

First, we must *turn to the truth of God* (vv. 8-9). The prophets in Babylon were telling the captives the things they wanted to hear, but that did not make those things true.

We might say that this was an early example of "feel-good" religion. It made the people feel good, but it did no good.

This kind of religion continues to thrive. Many decide what church they will attend on the basis of whether it makes them feel good. If the pastor talks about sin, coming judgment, and Christ as the only way of salvation, they hurry away. It doesn't occur to them to ask whether the pastor is telling the truth. They don't understand the purpose of religion that disturbs. It is for their good, just as it's for the good of the patient when the doctor tells him disturbing medical news.

Secondly, we must *turn to the thoughts of God* (v. 11).

Isn't it comforting to know that the Lord thinks about His people? The captives in Babylon must have thought the Lord had forgotten about them. This wasn't the case. The Lord says: "I know the thoughts that I think toward you."

Isn't it comforting to know that God has thoughts of peace about His people? The captives may have been saying: "Yes, God is thinking about us. He is thinking of ways to make us miserable."

But God told them it was not so. His thoughts were of "peace and not of evil." When God chastises His people, it isn't because He is mean and cruel but rather because He is kind and loving, and wants what is best for them.

Isn't it comforting to know that God thinks about the future?

God wanted the captives to know He had their future planned. Although the captivity wouldn't be short, it would definitely come to an end. When it did, God would restore them to their homeland.

Chastisement is never God's final word for His people. He chastises us to develop and mature us. Some day that process will be over, and God will bring us home to heaven.

Isn't it comforting to know that God's thinking about us can't be thwarted? The Jewish people were released from captivity just as the Lord promised, and all the promises He has regarding us will come true (Num. 23:19; Josh. 21:45).

Finally, our times of trouble should cause us to *turn to the throne of God* (vv. 12-13).

After promising to bring His people home, the Lord says: "Then you will call upon Me, and I will listen to you."

The word "then" doesn't refer to the time of their return home but rather to that time when the truth the Lord had just stated would come home to their hearts. In other words, when they realized that God was thinking about them and that He was thinking about their peace and about their future, they would then turn to Him in prayer. Knowing these things will surely drive us to prayer as well.

Are you troubled? Don't be. Take your troubles to the truth, the thoughts, and the throne of God; and then watch them melt away.

A Place and a Peace

From God's Word, the Bible...

"Let not your heart be troubled; you believe in God, believe also in Me. In My Father's house are many mansions; if it were not so, I would have told you. I go to prepare a place for you. And if I go and prepare a place for you, I will come again and receive you to Myself; that where I am, there you may be also. And where I go you know, and the way you know." Thomas said to Him, "Lord, we do not know where You are going, and how can we know the way?" Jesus said to him, "I am the way, the truth, and the life. No one comes to the Father except through Me."

John 14:1-6

Chapters 13 through 16 of John's Gospel are immeasurably precious to the people of God. They relate some of what Jesus said to His disciples on the night before He was crucified. Someone observed that dying words are sacred words, and the words of these chapters can well be called the dying words of Jesus. The cross is now scant hours away.

Jesus had told His disciples on previous occasions that He must be put to death. But on those occasions His words seemed distant and unreal. On this night, it was all painfully real, and the disciples were crushed with sorrow.

So we aren't surprised to read that Jesus twice urged them not to let their hearts be troubled (John 14:1,27). The first time He used those words was in connection with a *place*, and the second in connection with a *peace*. So Jesus was saying that there was no reason for them to be troubled and distraught because they had a place to go and a peace until they got there. What He said to those despondent men applies equally to Christians today. We have a place to go, and we can enjoy peace while we are on the journey.

The place that awaits us is described by Jesus as "My Father's House" (John 14:1).

The Father's House! That means it is home, and that means it is the place of love, warmth, security, and pleasure.

Heaven is the Christian's home, and that we must never forget. We always get into trouble when we try to make this world our home. Good old Matthew Henry used to say this world is a traveling place and not a stopping place. The little rural church in which I grew up would often have the children sing this chorus:

This world is not my home
I'm just a-passing though,
My treasures are laid up
Somewhere beyond the blue;
The angels beckon me
From heaven's open door,
And I can't feel at home
In this world anymore.

The Father's house, Jesus said, is the place of many mansions. We associate mansions with permanence. Here is how permanent the Father's House is: it lasts forever!

One of the disciples, Thomas, must have been saying to himself: "The Father's house! That sounds wonderful! If only we knew the way to get there!" Then he blurted it out: ". . .how can we know the way?"

Jesus replied: "I am the way, the truth, and the life. No one comes to the Father except through Me."

To get to the Father's house, we have to come to the Father, and to come to the Father, we have to come to Jesus. He, Jesus, is the One who said: "I go to prepare a place for you" (v. 2).

Some understand Jesus to be saying that He was going back to heaven, and there He would busy Himself with building mansions. They imagine Him running around heaven with blueprints, hammers, saws, and nails. But Jesus was talking about going to the cross. That is where He dealt with the thing that keeps us out of heaven—sin! On the cross, He paid its penalty, and, in so doing, flung the door of heaven open wide to all who trust in Him and in what He did on that cross. On the basis of His work on that cross, Jesus is in heaven today to make intercession for all those who come to God through Him (Heb. 7:25).

So Christians have a place to go, but they also have a peace while they wait to get to the place. Jesus promised to give His peace to His disciples (v. 27).

This world cannot give us peace. It holds before us pleasures, possessions, and positions of influence and says: "These things will give you peace."

But it is all an illusion. Real peace is spiritual peace. It is peace that comes from knowing one is right with God in this world and will be present with Him in the world to come. The world may wish us peace, but it can never give us this kind of peace. Spiritual peace comes only through faith in the redeeming work of the Lord Jesus Christ and in being in a right relationship with Him.

March 16

The Words of Jesus

FROM GOD'S WORD, THE BIBLE...

It is the Spirit who gives life; the flesh profits nothing. The words that I speak to you are spirit, and they are life.

....

JOHN 6:63

We have the words of many people from ancient times and countless words from countless people since those times. Some of these words are interesting and valuable; others are trivial and meaningless. Why give special attention to the words of Jesus? Why pay more attention to them than to the words of Aristotle, Plato, Socrates, Shakespeare or Mohammed?

The first reason is Jesus was a person like no other.

We frequently encounter the view that all religions are virtually the same, that one can be exchanged for another without any appreciable loss or gain. People who hold this view are astounded that Christians claim that Jesus alone is Lord and Savior. And oftentimes they are eager to dismiss us as biased fools.

Why do Christians hold this belief? The answer is, of course, the evidence that Jesus was precisely the person He claimed to be—God Himself in human flesh.

This assertion has been abundantly proven by:

- the miracles that Jesus performed
- the prophecies that He fulfilled
- His resurrection from the grave.

How do we know that these things occurred? They were recorded by men who either witnessed them or carefully researched them (Luke 1:1-4; John 1:14; 20:30-31; Acts 1:1-3; Heb. 2:3-4; 1 John 1:1-4). The words of Jesus, then, no matter how difficult and challenging they may be, must be heeded because they were spoken by the One who has been demonstrated to be the God-man.

We must go still further. We must pay attention to the words of Jesus because the very words themselves have a special quality about them. The people who heard Jesus speak testified to this (Matt. 7:28-29; 13:54; John 7:46).

Simon Peter gave testimony to this special power in an unforgettable way. After a huge multitude had decided that they could no longer follow Him, Jesus asked his original twelve disciples: "Do you also want to go away?" (John 6:67).

Simon responded: "Lord, to whom shall we go? You have the words of eternal life. Also we have come to believe and know that You are the Christ, the Son of the living God" (John 6:68-69).

Simon was echoing that which Jesus had spoken a moment earlier: "It is the Spirit who gives life; the flesh profits nothing. The words that I speak to you are spirit, and they are life" (John 6:63).

Simon agreed. He had heard in the words of Jesus the authentic ring of the way to eternal life.

Christians readily endorse what Simon Peter said. As we read the words of Jesus in Scripture, something within tells us that we are indeed reading special words, words that are genuine and true, and, yes, words that reveal the way to eternal life. And that way is the Lord Jesus Himself. When Jesus spoke about having eternal life, He spoke about the necessity of believing in Him (John 3:16; 5:39-40; 6:40,47).

As we connect the words of Jesus with eternal life, we can joyfully sing with Philip P. Bliss:

Christ, the blessed One, gives to all, Wonderful words of life;
Sinner, list to the loving call, Wonderful words of life;
All so freely given,
Wooing us to heaven.
Beautiful words, wonderful words, Wonderful words of life;
Beautiful words, wonderful words, Wonderful words of life.

Yet another reason to pay special heed to the words of Jesus is this: those words have stood the test of time.

Each Sunday, and on other days as well, millions and millions of people gather together to study the words of Jesus. This is no small thing! Numberless authors have left the world with wonderful words. But only the words of Jesus receive attention on this scale week after week, not to mention the attention they receive from individuals on a daily basis. This must be considered a fulfillment of these words:

The grass withers, the flower fades,
But the word of our God stands forever.
(Isa. 40:8)

The words of Jesus are in a category by themselves. No other words can begin to compare to them. Let us read them and heed them. If we do, we will land safely on heaven's shore, and there we will find that everything is just as He, Jesus, said (Luke 19:32; 22:13).

Quickly Forgotten, Forever Remembered

From God's Word, the Bible...

But Zion said, "The Lord has forsaken me,
And my Lord has forgotten me."
"Can a woman forget her nursing child,
And not have compassion on the son of her womb?
Surely they may forget, Yet I will not forget you.
See, I have inscribed you on the palms of My hands;
Your walls are continually before Me."

Isaiah 49:14-16

A college professor gives his new students a brief quiz. He first asks them to name their parents. Then he asks them to name their four grandparents. Finally, he asks them to name their eight great-grandparents.

As you would expect, the students have no trouble with the first two questions, but not one has been able to successfully answer the third.

Given these results, the professor concluded that we can expect our children and grandchildren to love us but our great grandchildren not to even know our names! So my five grandchildren are my last link to my being remembered in this world. How brief is our time on this earth and how brief is the remembrance of us when we are gone!

But for the Christian being forgotten in this world does not mean being totally forgotten. The Lord will always remember His people. Through His prophet Isaiah, the Lord said to His people:

Can a woman forget her nursing child,
And not have compassion on the son of her womb?
Surely they may forget,
Yet I will not forget you.
(Isa. 49:15)

The people would receive these words during a terrible time of crisis. Because of their sins they would be in captivity in Babylon. That would put them five hundred miles away from Jerusalem, and the captivity would last a very long time—seventy years. But neither distance nor time could make the Lord forget them. He says to them:

See, I have inscribed you on the palms of My hands;
Your walls are continually before Me.
(Isa. 49:16)

Just as it is impossible to forget the writing on the palms of our hands, so it is impossible for the Lord to forget His people. And this is no mere writing. The word "inscribed" means "engraved."

Didn't the Jews go into captivity because of sinful living? Yes. Were their sins not enough to cause God to completely forget them? No. Alexander Maclaren says: ". . .there is no sin that is strong enough to chill the divine love, or to erase us from the divine remembrance."[5]

And what about those walls? They refer to the walls of Jerusalem, and those walls were lying in ruins during those years of captivity. If someone had asked the Jewish captives there in Babylon to close their eyes and visualize the walls of Jerusalem, they would have said: "We see nothing but ruins." And they might very well have taken those ruins to mean that God had forgotten them. But where they saw ruins, God saw walls. Their sins, which had produced the ruins of Jerusalem, didn't mean that God had erased them from His memory. The fact that He saw future walls for Jerusalem meant He had not forgotten them

When the captivity came to an end (and it did come to an end, just as God promised), the Lord spoke to His people through the prophet Malachi. That would also be a time of great challenge. Wicked people would be so prospering and flourishing that it would cause the people of God to wonder if there was any point in serving the Lord (Mal. 2:17; 3:15). It would look as if God had forgotten to bless His faithful people and instead had chosen to bless the godless.

But God would not forget them. He keeps a book of remembrance that makes it impossible for Him to forget. In this world, His people are often treated with disdain. They are, as it were, thrown down into the mud to be trampled on. But in due time, God will pluck them out of the mire and will reveal them to be His precious jewels (Mal. 3:17). There is coming a day in which everyone will know that those who served the Lord in this life were wise to do so.

But how can we be sure that God never forgets His people? Let's go back to God having His people engraved on His hands. How can we be sure of this? We can be sure we are engraved on God's hands because of the hands of Jesus. God would never have allowed the hands of His Son to be nailed to the cross only to forget those who have trusted in Jesus and His redeeming death. Jesus' crucified hands are the proof that God's people are engraved on His hands.

Forgotten in this life? Very likely! Forgotten by God? Never!

5 Alexander Maclaren, *Expositions of Holy Scripture: Isaiah and Jeremiah*, Baker Book House, Grand Rapids, 1974, p. 12

March 18

A Message from Ahimaaz

FROM GOD'S WORD, THE BIBLE...

Now David was sitting between the two gates. And the watchman went up to the roof over the gate, to the wall, lifted his eyes and looked, and there was a man, running alone. Then the watchman cried out and told the king. And the king said, "If he is alone, there is news in his mouth." And he came rapidly and drew near. Then the watchman saw another man running, and the watchman called to the gatekeeper and said, "There is another man, running alone!" And the king said, "He also brings news."

FROM 2 SAMUEL 18:19-33

Ahimaaz could run. He wasn't just fast; he was very, very fast. If the Olympics had been in existence in his day, Ahimaaz would have been a gold medal winner in at least one event, and maybe in several.

It isn't surprising if you are having trouble remembering Ahimaaz. He isn't what we would call a major Bible character. He isn't in the same league as Abraham, Moses or David. He appears in only one chapter in the Bible, and only in the last half of that chapter. He falls into the category of obscure Bible characters.

Ahimaaz occupies such little space in the Bible that we might find ourselves wondering why he is even mentioned at all. The fact is, however, that he has a very important lesson to teach us. We might call him the minor man with a major message. What is that message? Let's wait for that.

Ahimaaz lived during that wretched time when King David's own son, Absalom, decided he wanted to be king. That meant he would have to overthrow his father, but that didn't matter to Absalom who was a thoroughly disgusting human being.

So Absalom gathered a following—a large following—and tried to take the kingdom. It almost succeeded. But God made sure it didn't. Absalom's army was defeated, and he was slain. Joab, the captain of David's army, had to dispatch a runner to carry the news to David. At this point we meet Ahimaaz. He begged Joab to choose him, but Joab chose a man the Bible simply calls "the Cushite." The Cushite began running, and Ahimaaz continued begging until Joab, out of sheer exasperation, finally said: "Run" (v. 23).

That was the word Ahimaaz wanted to hear, and off he went. It didn't matter that the Cushite had a head start. Ahimaaz was fast. He passed the Cushite and got to David first with the news that the battle had been won. But David wanted to know more than the outcome of the battle. He wanted to know what had become of Absalom. Ahimaaz either couldn't say or he wouldn't say. Maybe he couldn't say. Maybe he, Ahimaaz, was telling the truth when he said to David: "I saw a great tumult, but I did not know what it was about" (v. 29). Joab had plainly said to Ahimaaz: ". . .the king's son is dead" (v. 20), but it's possible that the excitable Ahimaaz didn't even hear those words.

So Ahimaaz, the faster runner, had to stand alongside David until the slower runner, the Cushite, arrived with the news David most needed to hear—the news about his son. The Cushite put it in these words: "May the enemies of my lord the king, and all who rise against you to do you harm, be as that young man is!" (v. 32).

David understood. His son was dead.

And now we are ready for that vitally important message that Ahimaaz has to teach us. Ahimaaz didn't do well in his running to David, but he does run out of this narrative to deliver a message to us. In this running he does very well indeed. The message of Ahimaaz is this: it doesn't matter how fast we run if we don't deliver the message people most need to hear.

The Bible gives us a message we all need to hear. It tells us God has given us certain laws, and about our failure to keep those laws. Furthermore, it warns us about that day in which each of us must stand before God. If we stand there in our sins, we will be driven from Him. But the good news is that we don't have to stand before God in our sins. Through His Son, Jesus, God has done everything necessary for our sins to be forgiven. That forgiveness will be ours if we truly repent of our sins and trust in Christ.

This is the message churches and pastors are called to deliver, but, sadly enough, many, like Ahimaaz, are failing. They are running very fast and being very energetic in providing various activities and promotions, but, again, it doesn't matter how fast we run if we don't deliver the message people need.

I think Ahimaaz was warm, energetic, outgoing, and vibrant. I think I would like him; but when it comes to the matter of delivering the needed message, I don't want to be like him. Let me be like the Cushite.

March 19

A Hymn Born in Heckling

FROM GOD'S WORD, THE BIBLE...

And when they crucified Him, they divided His garments, casting lots for them to determine what every man should take.
Now it was the third hour, and they crucified Him. And the inscription of His accusation was written above:
THE KING OF THE JEWS.
With Him they also crucified two robbers, one on His right and the other on His left. So the Scripture was fulfilled which says, "And He was numbered with the transgressors."
And those who passed by blasphemed Him, wagging their heads and saying, "Aha! You who destroy the temple and build it in three days, save Yourself, and come down from the cross!"

MARK 15:24-31

The year was 1912. Evangelist George Bennard was preaching in a gospel crusade in Michigan. As he preached one night, he was continually heckled by a group of young people.

Shocked and deeply troubled by the contempt these young people expressed toward the gospel, Bennard wrote the first verse of *The Old Rugged Cross*:

On a hill far away
Stood an old rugged cross
The emblem of suffering and shame
And I love that old cross
Where the dearest and best
For a world of lost sinners was slain.

A few months later, Bennard added the last three verses of the hymn. In three of the four verses, he admits the disdain so many feel about the message of the cross. In verse one, the cross is the emblem of "shame." In verse two, it is "despised by the world." In verse four, it is the object of "shame and reproach."

With each of his candid acknowledgments of the world's hatred for the cross, Bennard gives a ringing affirmation of his esteem for it. In verse one, he says: "I love that old cross." In verse two, he declares that the cross holds "a wondrous attraction" for him. In verse three, he affirms that he sees "a wonderful beauty" in that cross. In verse four, he firmly resolves to "ever be true" to the cross and to "gladly bear" the "shame and reproach" connected with it.

In the chorus, he pledges to "cherish" the cross and to "cling" to it until that day on which he will "exchange it for a crown."

One writer understands Bennard to be suggesting that when believers get to heaven they will exchange what occurred on the cross so that they might receive a crown. Is this writer saying that believers in heaven will no longer need to think about the cross? I hope not!

That certainly is not what Bennard is saying. Rather he is declaring that in heaven, Christians will no longer have to endure the ridicule, the disdain, and the mockery that their love for the cross so often brings them in this life. In heaven they will finally exchange all of that for a crown. By the way, the "trophies" that Bennard says he will "lay down" refer to the scars and wounds he would receive in this life from those who despise the cross. Just as a soldier might consider his wounds to be "trophies" of war, so the Christian regards whatever wounds he receives for loving the cross not as wounds at all but rather as trophies. In heaven they will be laid down. No one in heaven will ever be wounded or scarred for loving the cross.

In heaven there will be no cross-haters, only cross-lovers because everyone there will realize that he or she is there by virtue of that cross. In heaven believers will finally be all done with contempt for the cross and will wear the crown of victory.

It's not a good thing that Bennard was heckled so many years ago, but I'm glad that he was. That heckling prompted him to write a hymn that has brought tremendous blessing to millions.

Bennard certainly wasn't the first Christian to be heckled, and he wasn't the last. The heckling goes on today—with increasing intensity and ferocity, it seems. The more the hatred of the cross grows, the more we should appreciate Bennard's hymn. May God be pleased to use its words to instill in our hearts the fervent desire to "cherish" the cross and to "cling" to it! It will certainly be costly to do so, but we must be willing to pay the price, remembering all the while that Jesus paid a much greater price for us when He died on that cross.

To the old rugged cross
I will ever be true,
Its shame and reproach gladly bear;
Then He'll call me someday
To my home far away,
Where His glory forever I'll share.
So I'll cherish the old rugged cross
Till my trophies at last I lay down;
I will cling to the old rugged cross
And exchange it some day for a crown.

The Unfailing Friend

FROM GOD'S WORD, THE BIBLE...

A man who has friends must himself be friendly,
But there is a friend who sticks closer than a brother.

PROVERBS 18:24

Greater love has no one than this, than to lay down one's life for his friends. You are My friends if you do whatever I command you. No longer do I call you servants, for a servant does not know what his master is doing; but I have called you friends, for all things that I heard from My Father I have made known to you.

FROM JOHN 15:9-17

The *Andy Griffith Show* was produced in television's wholesome days. That was many years ago. In one episode, Andy, the sheriff of Mayberry, arrests a beautiful woman for speeding. It's obvious that she was not speeding a little but a lot. Barney, Floyd, and Opie were with Andy when the woman so flagrantly flaunted the law, but she so charmed them that they failed to give clear testimony regarding her violation. Opie's wavering could be forgiven. But there was no excuse for Barney and Floyd. At the end of the trial, Andy "congratulates" the woman for swaying the two men that he thought would "never leave" his side.

The episode ends well. The woman recognized that she had been wrong and paid her fine. And Andy's friendship with Barney and Floyd was repaired.

Most of us could write a similar script. We have to change the names and the circumstances, but the central plot—friend turning against friend—would remain the same. We know about this. We know about the pain it brings, and that pain is almost unbearable.

Experiencing the heartache of faithless friends should help us appreciate the friend who never fails. Who is that? Joseph M. Scriven supplies the answer:

What a friend we have in Jesus,
All our sins and griefs to bear!
What a privilege to carry,
Everything to God in prayer!

We know Scriven was no stranger to heartache. In 1845 he stood in stunned amazement as the body of his fiancée was lifted out of the murky waters of a lake. They were supposed to be married the next day.

In 1855 his mother was stricken with serious illness. Far from home and with no money to make the trip, Scriven wrote the lines of *What a Friend We Have in Jesus* and sent them to her.

In 1860 he lost another fiancée—this time to tuberculosis.

Two fiancées. Two deaths. A sick mother. I'd say Scriven knew about heartache. And evidently he also had friends turn against him. In the third verse he raises this question:

Do thy friends despise, forsake thee?

But Scriven found the answer for all his heartaches, including the loss of friends:

Take it to the Lord in prayer.
In His arms He'll take and shield Thee;
Thou wilt find a solace there.

The friendship of Jesus! This is a friendship without measure, without change, and without end. Our earthly friendships are not without measure. There is a limit to them. They are not without change. Sometimes they cool. They are not without end. Jesus' friendship is different. There is none like it.

Jesus says: "Greater love has no one than this, than to lay down one's life for his friends" (John 15:13).

And this is exactly what Jesus did for His people. He laid down His life on the cross for them. I sometimes think we do not fully appreciate this. We are all familiar with stories about people laying down their lives for their friends. But what Jesus did on the cross is in a completely different category. If you were to give up your life to save a friend, it would certainly be a noble act, but you would only be speeding up what is inevitable because you are already destined to die. But Jesus didn't have to die. As God, He was not subject to death. In order to die He had to take our humanity. In dying for us, He came to do what He did not have to do.

In addition to that, the kind of death Jesus died was entirely different than any other kind of death. In other words, Jesus' death was far more than a physical phenomenon. On the cross, He experienced an eternity's worth of God-forsakenness so His friends would never have to experience it.

Thank God for the friendship of Jesus! Other friendships may fail, but His never will. It begins in this life for all who come to Him in repentance and faith, and it will continue undimmed and undiminished through the ceaseless ages of eternity. If you have the friendship of Jesus, you have a Friend who will never leave your side (Heb. 13:5).

March 21

No Continuing City

From God's Word, the Bible...

For here we have no continuing city, but we seek the one to come.

Hebrews 13:14

The author of Hebrews wrote his letter to Jews who had professed faith in the Lord Jesus Christ. All would seem to be well, but these people were in trouble. Their profession of faith had brought suffering their way. Some of their number had already been driven out of their much-loved city of Jerusalem. Others were expecting the same to happen to them.

This author wrote to encourage them. He reminded them that Jesus had been driven out of Jerusalem to Golgotha, where He died on the cross. If Jesus was willing to do that for them, they should regard being driven out of Jerusalem for His cause as a small sacrifice indeed (Heb. 13:12-13).

Having made that argument, the author proceeds to tell them that they were mistaken to attach so much significance to the city of Jerusalem. It was not "a continuing city," and neither is any other city in this world.

This brief text never fails to warm and encourage my heart. I see a threefold division in it: a *fact*, a *promise* and a *duty*. The fact is one which no one can deny, the promise is one which no one should deny, but the duty is one which many do deny.

The *fact* which no one can deny is what I've already mentioned. Here we have no continuing city. This city, or this world, doesn't last. So we are wise not to allow ourselves to get too attached to it. It doesn't last because we don't continue in it. We die (Heb. 9:27). And the city itself will finally die. The Apostle John writes: "And the world is passing away, and the lust of it; but he who does the will of God abides forever" (1 John 2:17).

This same point is brought powerfully home in Revelation 18:21-24. There this world is pictured as another city—Babylon. And her eventual ruin is driven home in the English Standard Version rendering by a phrase that appears six times in verses 21-23. It is the phrase "no more." Like a trip hammer, it sounds: No more, no more, no more. . . . Babylon is "no more," and her music (v. 22), arts and crafts (v. 22), industry (v. 23), light (v. 23), and the joy of human relationships (v. 23) are "no more."

If we feel as sharply as we should the temporariness of this world, we will appreciate God's *promise*. It is a promise no one should deny. It is implied in our text by the words "the one to come." The point is clear. There is a lasting city to come. The Apostle Peter says: ". . .we, according to His promise, look for new heavens and a new earth in which righteousness dwells" (2 Peter 3:13).

The earthly Jerusalem will not last, but God has promised a New Jerusalem that will last (Rev. 21:1-2).

That phrase "no more" that so somberly describes the end of this world is used in Revelation 21 and 22 to gloriously describe what awaits the children of God. There will be "no more" sea, death, sorrow, crying, pain or curse.

We can confidently await the coming of the New Jerusalem because God has promised it, and God cannot lie (Titus 1:2).

So our *duty*—and our privilege—is to seek that city which is to come. We seek it by repenting of our sins and by trusting in Christ and His redeeming work on the cross. We seek it by daily living with the expectation that it will come and by ordering our lives in such a way that we show that we are already citizens of that better, lasting city. Abraham and other people of faith diligently sought it (Heb. 11:10,13-16), and we should seek it as well. This is our duty, but, alas, it is one which so many deny. They do not seek the lasting city because they are so enamored and infatuated with the passing city. Their folly will at last become clear, but when it is does it will be too late.

May God help each of us to be clearheaded and clear-sighted enough to see this world for what it is and that better world God has promised and to live now for that better world.

David Couldn't Miss, but We Can

From God's Word, the Bible...

Then David put his hand in his bag and took out a stone; and he slung it and struck the Philistine in his forehead, so that the stone sank into his forehead, and he fell on his face to the earth. So David prevailed over the Philistine with a sling and a stone, and struck the Philistine and killed him. But there was no sword in the hand of David.

I Samuel 17:49-50

When nine-feet tall Goliath was tauntingly challenging the soldiers of the Israelite army, they cringed and cowered. Each one was probably saying of Goliath: "He's too big to hit!" When David saw him, he might very well have said: "He's too big to miss!"

It's true. David couldn't miss when he hurled his first stone at Goliath. But it wasn't because Goliath was so big. It was rather because that stone was guided with laser-precision by the unseen hand of the sovereign God. That stone hit Goliath in the head, he fell to the ground, and David used Goliath's own sword to behead him.

While David couldn't miss, we can. We can look right over the main thing God wants this incident to convey. This story is often used to suggest ways in which we can kill the giant problems that life can bring our way.

The trend in the last several years has been to look for life-lessons in the stories of the Old Testament. We ought to be more concerned about looking for Lord-lessons. I say this because of what the Lord Jesus Himself said to His disciples (see Luke 24:27, 44).

With that principle in place, we have to say that the account of David and Goliath is intended to point us to the Lord Jesus. Where do we find Him in this account? He is the greater David who defeated a greater Goliath to achieve a greater deliverance.

Think about the greater Goliath. The Goliath of the Philistines was a formidable foe indeed—nine feet tall with armor weighing 125 pounds. He hated the Israelites and desired nothing more than to enslave and destroy them.

As great as Goliath was, he could not begin to compare to the enemy of all mankind—Satan! Yes, he is a real person, and his desire is to first enslave and finally destroy the souls of individuals. Goliath had his sword and spear. Satan's master weapon is deception. He deceives people about themselves (telling them that they aren't sinners or that sin is not serious) and about God (telling them He doesn't exist or if He does, He will not judge sin).

That brings us to the greater David. David stepped forward as the champion of his people when they were both helpless and hopeless. Spurning Saul's heavy armor, David went out to meet the giant with his shepherd's sling and five smooth stones. It would seem that there was no way for him to succeed. But succeed he did.

Jesus is our champion. As David defeated Goliath on behalf of his own people, so Christ has defeated Satan on behalf of His own people. Jesus achieved victory for us by using an even more unlikely instrument than David's sling and stones. Jesus' instrument of victory was a Roman cross! That cross defeated Satan (Col. 2:15). The only way Satan's hold on us could be broken was for sin's hold on us to be broken. And the only way sin's hold on us could be broken was for its penalty to be paid. That is what Jesus did on the cross. He paid the penalty for sin so all who believe in Him will not have to pay it themselves.

The author of Hebrews calls his readers to rejoice that "through death" the Lord Jesus destroys him "who had the power of death, that is, the devil" and He, Jesus, releases those who were "subject to bondage" (Heb. 2:14-15).

What Jesus did on the cross achieves a far greater deliverance than David achieved for the Israelites. Their deliverance was temporal and temporary. It was still possible for another enemy to arise to defeat and enslave them. The deliverance provided by Jesus is eternal. Those who trust in Him can never be enslaved by Satan again. All who believe in the Lord Jesus are delivered from slavery to Satan in this life and in the life to come.

Is it okay to look for life-lessons in the story of David and Goliath? Yes, but we should always treat such lessons as secondary. The primary thing is the work of Jesus. Let's be sure not to miss that!

God's Face Hidden and Unhidden

From God's Word, the Bible...

"According to their uncleanness and according to their transgressions I have dealt with them, and hidden My face from them."

"And I will not hide My face from them anymore; for I shall have poured out My Spirit on the house of Israel," says the Lord God.

From Ezekiel 39:21-29

It's not something we like to think about, but it is a reality. I'm talking about God hiding His face from His people.

We have one example of it in the passage before us. Ezekiel had been called by God to prophesy to the people of God who were in captivity in Babylon.

Why did God send His people into captivity? He tells us very plainly: ". . .the house of Israel went into captivity for their iniquity; because they were unfaithful to Me, therefore I hid My face from them" (v. 23).

God also says: "According to their uncleanness and according to their transgressions I have dealt with them, and hidden My face from them" (v. 24).

In sending His people into captivity, God was simply carrying out the very thing He said He would do if His people forsook Him and broke His covenant: "Then My anger shall be aroused against them in that day, and I will forsake them, and I will hide My face from them" (Deut. 31:17).

God proceeds to say: "And I will surely hide My face in that day because of all the evil which they have done, in that they have turned to other gods" (Deut. 31:18).

What are the sins of today's church that are causing God to hide His face from her? Is it refusing to preach the truth about sin and judgment to come in order to build a religious empire? Is it pride? Is it idolatry? Is it dissension and rivalry?

And what about us as individuals? What are our sins? What are we doing to hide God's face? What are we failing to do?

God doesn't hide His face from His people to be cruel and mean to them. He does it to correct them. In Ezekiel 39 we find the Lord anticipating that day when His correction of His people would be complete. Here is what He says: ". . .I will not hide My face from them anymore; for I shall have poured out My Spirit on the house of Israel. . ." (v. 39).

It is vital that we make this connection—the opposite of God hiding His face is Him pouring out His Spirit.

To say God is hiding His face is to say that He is not pouring out His Spirit. And to say God is not pouring out His Spirit is to say that nothing of any value can be accomplished in our churches as long as the Spirit is withheld.

What are God's people to do when He is hiding His face from them? What must we do if are to enjoy once again the unhidden face of God? Here is another way to put it: If God is hiding His face from His people, what does He expect them to do?

The answer, I suggest, is supplied in these words that David spoke to God:

When You said, "Seek My face,"
My heart said to You,
"Your face, LORD, I will seek."
(Ps. 27:8)

The answer is plain to see. If God is hiding His face from us, He wants us to seek His face. If our sins cause Him to hide His face, then to seek His face means we must turn from our sins in true repentance. Are we doing this? Are we seeking God's face through heartfelt repentance, or are we content to go along as we are?

Although Christians frequently fail, they never have to be concerned about losing their salvation. In other words, they never have to be concerned about God hiding His face from them in eternity (Rev. 22:3-5). And what's the reason God's people don't have to fear Him hiding His face from them in eternity? It's because He hid His face from Jesus when He, Jesus, was on the cross. If God hides His face from sin and Jesus became sin for us (2 Cor. 5:21), God had to hide His face from Jesus. If we turn from our sins and trust in the Lord Jesus, it will be our enormous privilege to "see His face" throughout eternity (Rev. 22:4).

A Rich Dwelling

From God's Word, the Bible...

Let the word of Christ dwell in you richly in all wisdom, teaching and admonishing one another in psalms and hymns and spiritual songs, singing with grace in your hearts to the Lord.

Colossians 3:16

In this text the Apostle Paul urges his readers to let the Word of Christ dwell "richly" within them.

We find the word of Christ in the Bible. The Bible consists of many, many words, but it is essentially one word. It has one message, and that is the message of Christ. It is the Word of God, and since Christ is God, it is also the Word of Christ. The Bible is Christ speaking about Christ!

In the Bible the Lord Jesus Christ tells us that God, our Creator, is holy and righteous, and He demands that we have perfect righteousness or He will not admit us into heaven (Rev. 21:27). The Lord Jesus also tells us that we do not have the righteousness that God requires. Each of us has broken God's laws time after time. God demands righteousness, and we don't have it. Thankfully, the Lord Jesus tells us about Himself. He tells us that He does have the righteousness God demands, and His righteousness can be counted as ours if we will trust Him as our Lord and Savior. What about all our sins? The Lord Jesus tells us in the Bible that His death on the cross paid the penalty for those who believe. Here is Christianity in a nutshell—Jesus got our sins, and we get His righteousness.

It should be obvious to us that we have in the Bible an immeasurable treasure. It's no wonder David said to the Lord:

I have rejoiced in the way of Your testimonies,
As much as in all riches.
(Ps. 119:14)

The law of Your mouth is better to me
Than thousands of shekels of gold and silver.
(Ps. 119:72)

I rejoice at Your word, As one who finds great treasure.
(Ps. 119:162)

The question is not whether we have enormous riches in the Bible. It is rather whether we are letting those riches dwell richly in us. It is not enough, however, to hold the Bible in our hands. We must hold it in our hearts, treasuring it for its richness.

So how do we let the Word of Christ dwell richly within? It's obvious that we must read it, but we must ever be on guard against the tendency to merely read words. How easy it is for us to do our daily Bible reading only to come away without being able to tell anyone what we read. To read the Bible well, we have to read it:

- confidently, knowing it is true and dependable (Ps. 119:142,151,160; 2 Tim. 3:16; 2 Peter 1:21)
- joyfully (Ps. 119:14,162; Jer. 15:16)
- diligently (Acts 17:11; 2 Tim. 2:15)
- reverently (Ps. 119:161; Isa. 66:2,5)
- Christocentrically, that is, looking for the Lord Jesus who is its sub-ject and focus (Luke 24:27,44-45; John 5:39; Acts 8:35; 2 Tim. 3:14-15)
- experientially (Is there a promise for me to believe? A command for me to obey? An example for me to copy?)

Furthermore, if we are to have the Bible dwelling richly within us, we must give priority to regularly attending public worship services in which the message of the Bible is faithfully preached and taught. But it's not enough to merely park our bodies on church pews. We must discipline ourselves to listen—really listen—to the preaching and teaching of God's Word, saying to the Lord: "Speak, for Your servant hears" (1 Sam. 3:10).

Those of us who have been blessed to be part of God-honoring, Christ-exalting, Bible-preaching churches for years should constantly remind ourselves that our blessing can become our curse. Familiarity with the Scriptures is a blessing, but when we allow that familiarity to cause us not to eagerly listen, it is a curse. We should come to each event of the preaching and teaching of the Word as if we were hearing it for the first time.

I want to be rich, but I hope I know what it is to be rich. It is not a matter of what I dwell in but rather what dwells in me, and to what degree it dwells there.

Lord, may Your Word dwell richly in me.

What About Christophobia?

From God's Word, the Bible...

Beloved, I beg you as sojourners and pilgrims, abstain from fleshly lusts which war against the soul, having your conduct honorable among the Gentiles, that when they speak against you as evildoers, they may, by your good works which they observe, glorify God in the day of visitation.

1 Peter 2:11-12

(Read 1 Peter 3:8-17 and 1 Peter 4:12-19 for this meditation, too.)

Lots of "phobias" are being tossed around these days—Islamaphobia, homophobia, xenophobia, to mention just a few such terms.

Express a viewpoint that is out of keeping with the political correctness of our day, and you will likely find yourself labeled as a "phobe" of one kind or another, and as far as the labelers are concerned, nothing could possibly be worse. And, of course, those who are so eager to apply the "phobe" tag to others congratulate themselves on being free from such phobias. But are they?

The same people who warn us about various phobias are ever vigilant to warn us about hatred and hate crimes.

There is one phobia that appears to be growing by leaps and bounds, but it is never mentioned. It is Christophobia, that is, fear of Christianity or fear of Christians. Those who enjoy tossing the phobia label around have no interest in Christophobia. Could it be that they are Christophobes?

And many of those who lecture us about hatred don't hesitate to express their hatred for Christians and Christianity. Is there a double standard at work here?

Hatred toward any individual or group is obviously wrong, and Christians oppose it. But we have reached the point where no one can disagree with any aspect of the political correctness of our day without being tagged as a hater. Disagreement is now hatred!

Interestingly enough, many who hate Christianity openly admit it. But they argue that their hatred is justified. Associating Christianity with oppression of African-Americans, women, and homosexuals, they believe that they can't champion the rights of those groups without hating Christianity. Have Christians been guilty of such oppressions? It is more correct to say that *professing* Christians have been guilty of many heinous things, but one of the fundamental teachings of the Bible is that not all who profess to be Christians are, in fact, what they profess. The haters of Christianity never make that distinction. Their hatred for the Christian faith is such that they will seize the wrong thinking and wrongdoing of a professing Christian and attribute the same to all Christians. They tar all with the same brush.

This isn't to say that even true Christians are perfect in all their views and acts. They aren't. But as believers in Christ grow in their understanding of His teachings, they come to see their errors and endeavor to correct them.

Many of the Christophobes of our day are simply misinformed. They associate Christianity with oppression, but they have never bothered to thoroughly research what Christians have done to fight oppression, relieve suffering, and attain equality. They don't delve into such matters because that would destroy their narrative, and they are very eager to maintain that narrative.

How are Christians to respond to the increasing number of Christophobes in our day? We need to be very careful to live in a Christlike manner. We need to seek to disarm and discredit our critics by engaging in such good conduct that they will find it hard to apply their labels and express their hatred.

And in the hatred of Christianity, we can and should find reason to be grateful. Grateful? Yes! It is a delicious irony that those who hate Christianity show by that very hatred that Christianity is true. Jesus clearly predicted that His followers would be hated (John 15:18-25), and every hateful word and deed that comes our way proves those words to be true.

An old story has soldiers shooting their arrows skyward because they were angry with the gods, only to have those arrows fall on their own heads. So the hatred of Christianity has a way of coming back on those who hate it.

Finally, we must also respond to the hatred of Christians by looking forward to that day when the Lord Jesus Christ and those who know Him will be fully vindicated. These are days in which we should cling tenaciously to these words: "These will make war with the Lamb, and the Lamb will overcome them, for He is Lord of lords and King of kings; and those who are with Him are called, chosen, and faithful" (Rev. 17:14).

While we wait for that day of victory, let's be thankful we can suffer in some measure for the Christ who suffered so much to make the victory a reality.

Broken Hearts, Numbered Stars

FROM GOD'S WORD, THE BIBLE...

Praise the LORD!
For it is good to sing praises to our God;
For it is pleasant, and praise is beautiful.
The LORD builds up Jerusalem;
He gathers together the outcasts of Israel.
He heals the brokenhearted
And binds up their wounds.
He counts the number of the stars;
He calls them all by name.
Great is our Lord, and mighty in power;
His understanding is infinite.
The LORD lifts up the humble;
He casts the wicked down to the ground.

PSALM 147:1-6

The old preacher J.C. Ryle used to say: "Heart-trouble is the commonest thing in the world."[6] He was not talking about the heart as a physical organ. He was talking about sorrow of heart or brokenheartedness.

The original readers of Psalm 147 knew about the broken heart. They were in captivity in Babylon. Their city, the city of Jerusalem, was in ruins. The beautiful temple built by Solomon was a pile of rubble. Homes were gone. Family members were separated. The question that frequently echoed in their heads was this: "Does God care?"

This psalmist wrote to give them the answer. He assured them that God would gather them, that is, bring them home, and in doing so would heal their broken hearts.

This author sets forth an unusual treatment for broken hearts. We can call it the therapy of the stars. Have you noticed it? Immediately after telling them that God heals the brokenhearted, he says God numbers the stars. How does he get from the former to the latter?

Think about the stars. If we could take a ride on a beam of light, we would be traveling 186,000 miles per second. That means we would go around the earth seven times each second. If we could ride our beam for 6,000 years, we would be only one-tenth of the way across our galaxy, and, there are billions of galaxies. All of this led the psalmist to say:

6 *Expository Thoughts on John, vol. 3*, Edinburgh, The Banner of Truth Trust, p.55

Great is our Lord, and mighty in power; His understanding is infinite.
(Ps. 147:5)

The point is that our God is more than sufficient for healing our broken hearts.

Someone might say: "That doesn't help at all. It only makes me feel like an insignificant speck. It makes me feel as if God doesn't know about my broken heart."

But we are not through with the therapy of the stars. The psalmist assures us that God knows the stars individually—"He calls them all by name" (v. 4). Countless numbers of stars—gazillions of them—and God knows each one and has named each of them. If God knows each star by name, why should we doubt that he knows all about us?

The therapy of the stars is great—God is sufficient for us and God has individual knowledge of us. But it must finally give way to the therapy of the cross. Christians should not doubt that God knows and cares for His brokenhearted people because of the cross. He put His Son there to provide healing for the worst problem of all—the guilt of our sins. If God has already demonstrated on the cross His care for the greatest of our problems, how can we doubt that He cares about all our lesser problems?

Then there is that nasty question that is always hanging on the edge of any discussion about God's people having broken hearts. If God is as great as this psalmist says, He could obviously prevent His people from ever being brokenhearted. So why does God allow our hearts to be broken?

I'm sure that Joseph wondered why God allowed him to experience the brokenheartedness of being hated by his brothers, sold into slavery, and falsely accused and imprisoned. But while it didn't make sense to him at the time, he was able to say to his brothers at the end: "But as for you, you meant evil against me; but God meant it for good. . ." (Gen. 50:20)

We may not get to see God's purpose come full circle in this life as Joseph did. We may live out our lives with our whys. Let's always remember that final healing for broken hearts takes place in heaven. There we will learn why God worked in our lives as He did, and there it will all make perfect sense.

Trials dark on every hand,
And we cannot understand,
All the ways that God would lead us
To that blessed promised land;
But He'll guide us with His eye,
And we'll follow till we die;
We will understand it better by and by.
(Charles A. Tindley)

March 27

Is Christianity Boring?

FROM GOD'S WORD, THE BIBLE...

...for the Son of Man has come to seek and to save that which was lost.

LUKE 19:10

Lots of people, especially young people, refuse to attend church services because they find such services to be boring. So, the thinking goes, it's up to church leaders to get "boring" out of church. The best way to do so? The answer seems to be to replace it, "boring," with "entertaining."

In the effort to swap the one for the other, all kinds of things are being done. One pastor even preached in his pajamas! Are we really to believe that the sight of a pastor in pajamas caused many in the congregation to say: "Oh, good, the preacher is in his pajamas! Now I'm not bored!"

We have reached the point where all kinds of outlandish behavior is being condoned in churches in the interest of fighting boredom and making Christianity relevant and interesting.

Think about it! Christianity as it is presented in the Bible—and there is no other kind—isn't interesting. It's boring, and it's up to us to rescue it.

The syllogism driving many church leaders these days is as follows:

- Christianity is boring.
- People don't want to be bored.
- Christianity must be changed.

But this is a sorry syllogism. It doesn't even get off the ground. Its first premise is faulty. Christianity isn't boring. Those who find it to be so only reveal that they don't understand it.

What is Christianity? It is God's rescue mission. It is God rescuing sinners from the peril awaiting them.

Rescue from peril is not boring. When a fireman bursts into fire and smoke to rescue a woman, she doesn't say, "That was certainly boring." When a lifeguard saves a man from drowning, he doesn't say, "That was terribly boring."

We aren't bored when our personal survival or wellbeing is at stake. If you had handed me a paper dealing with skull fractures several years ago, I would have said: "I find this to be very boring." But then I suffered a skull fracture, and, guess what, I got very interested in skull fractures. What changed? My wellbeing wouldn't have been at stake at the time you handed me the paper, but it was when I had the skull fracture.

The fire, the rolling waves, and the skull fracture are serious perils, but they can't begin to compare to the one facing the sinner. That is the greatest peril of all. It is the peril of "flaming fire" in "everlasting destruction" (2 Thess. 1:8,9). It is the peril of weeping and gnashing of teeth (Matt. 13:42,50). It is the peril of the darkest darkness imaginable (Jude 13).

Do our sins really merit such things? Consider this: all sin is directed against the infinite God, and we have all sinned time after time without regard to God's warnings. What is appropriate punishment for numberless sins against an infinite person who has warned us again and again?

Some are ever eager to diminish the Bible's teachings on eternal peril by suggesting that the fire, the darkness, and the wailing constitute figurative language. But what kind of reality is it that requires such language to describe it? It must be a horrible reality indeed.

The good news is that the God against whom we have sinned rescues sinners from their peril. He sent His Son, the Lord Jesus Christ, to this earth in our humanity. Jesus came on a rescue mission. On the cross He paid the penalty that sinners deserve so they don't have to pay that same penalty. He endured the wrath of God in the place of all who will trust in Him. People who describe Christianity as boring only reveal that they have never understood God or what Jesus did on the cross. That assessment of the Christian faith tells us a lot more about them than it tells us about Christianity.

Christianity is God loving people who have spat in His face and offended Him again and again despite all the goodness He has shown to them. Let me personalize it. It is God Himself rescuing me from hell by taking my hell in the person of His Son. Because of what God has done, I no longer have to fear condemnation but wait with eager anticipation the glory of heaven. If that is boring, please count me among the bored.

March 28

My Favorite Words

From God's Word, the Bible...

But God, who is rich in mercy, because of His great love with which He loved us, even when we were dead in trespasses, made us alive together with Christ (by grace you have been saved), and raised us up together, and made us sit together in the heavenly places in Christ Jesus, that in the ages to come He might show the exceeding riches of His grace in His kindness toward us in Christ Jesus.

Ephesians 2:4-7

It is not unusual to hear people speak about a favorite color, a favorite place, a favorite song or a favorite food. We may even hear someone refer to a favorite uncle, aunt or cousin. We almost never hear anyone talk about a favorite word or words.

I can't say I have a favorite color, place, food or relative, but I do have favorite words. At the top of the list is the word *grace*. As far as I'm concerned, it is the queen of words. I'm not referring to the word as it is often used. If someone exhibits unusual elegance or poise, that person may be described as having "grace." While I certainly do not object to the word being used in that way, it is not what I have in mind. I'm referring rather to the grace of God in the matter of salvation for sinners.

What is grace? It is God freely bestowing on sinners everything they need to be forgiven of their sins and to be in a right standing with Him. It is God refusing to give to sinners what they deserve and giving them what they don't deserve. Grace is God doing the following:

- setting His heart on sinners even before the world began;
- providing in Christ the righteousness sinners don't have and payment for the sins they do have;
- working in their minds and hearts so they can receive Christ and what He has done;
- causing them to grow and mature so they conform more and more to the image of Christ;
- preserving them in their faith;
- bringing them safely home to glory.

Some think of salvation in terms of God doing His part and us doing our part; but grace emphasizes that there is only one part to salvation, and it is God's.

Propitiation is another of my favorite words. It takes us to the very heart of what the Lord Jesus did on the cross. There He propitiated, that is He satisfied or appeased, the wrath of God.

I often find myself thinking that the main thing people don't know about God is that He is holy. Or perhaps they don't understand what that means. Yes, it means God is free from all moral failure or blemish, but it also means He can't simply ignore sin. The Bible speaks of God's deep aversion to sin. It speaks of God "burning" in anger against it and "vomiting" at the sight of it.

God has real wrath against sinners. Before He can enter into a relationship with them, that wrath has to be satisfied. Jesus went to the cross for the express purpose of satisfying that wrath. The wrath of God fell on Jesus there on the cross, and there is no wrath now for those who repent of their sins and trust in the Lord Jesus Christ. Keith Getty puts it in these words:

This, the pow'r of the cross:
Christ became sin for us;
Took the blame, bore the wrath –
We stand forgiven at the cross.

This, the pow'r of the cross:
Son of God—slain for us.
What a love! What a cost!
We stand forgiven at the cross.

I have yet another word to add to the list of my favorite words. It is *mediator*. A mediator is one who steps between parties in conflict and makes peace. Jesus is our mediator, and He is the only possible mediator (1 Tim. 2:5). He is the God-man, fully God and fully man at one and the same time. So in the conflict between God and man, He can fully represent both. As God, He provided the redemption we need. As man, He received what our sins deserve.

Grace! Propitiation! Mediator! What marvelous words! Because of them we can have salvation. I love those words, but, come to think of it, there may be one word I love more—*saved*!

I've found a Friend, who is all to me,
His love is ever true;
I love to tell how He lifted me
And what His grace can do for you.
Saved by His pow'r divine,
Saved to new life sublime!
Life now is sweet and my joy is complete,
For I'm saved, saved, saved!
(Jack P. Scholfield)

March 29

That Great Thing

From God's Word, the Bible...

For I determined not to know anything among you except Jesus Christ and Him crucified.

But God forbid that I should boast except in the cross of our Lord Jesus Christ, by whom the world has been crucified to me, and I to the world.

1 Corinthians 2:2; Galatians 6:14

If you were asked to name the one great thing in your life, what would you say? What is that one thing that dominates and dwarfs all other things? What is the thing that you live for?

Many would not hesitate to name their family or their health or their financial wellbeing as their one great thing. Less discerning people might name sports or sexual pleasure or dining on fine food.

In his hymn *Ask Ye What Great Thing I Know*, Johann C. Schwedler (1672-1730) invites us to ask him to name his great thing. "Go ahead and ask me," he says. "Yes," he says, "ask me to name the thing that 'delights and stirs me so.'"

Have you ever seen a child so eager to answer a question that he or she begs the teacher to call on him or her?

Schwedler is like that child. He wants us to ask because he is ever so eager to give us his answer. He's afraid that we won't ask, but one gets the impression from his hymn that he would tell us even if we didn't ask.

So we give in to his eagerness. "Okay, Schwedler, we'll bite. Anything to get you to stop waving your arms at us and jumping up and down! What is your great thing?"

And Schwedler, relieved that we have finally asked, says—are you ready for this?—"Jesus Christ, the crucified."

This is Schwedler's great thing? A Jewish carpenter turned rabbi hanging on a Roman cross about 2,000 years ago? That's the great thing? Schwedler must have been out of his mind!

Was Schwedler crazy, or is it possible that he saw something in the cross of Jesus that most have never seen, something of such amazing significance that if they were to see it, they would join Schwedler in naming it as their great thing? And what did Schwedler see? He tells us that the cross was the place where Jesus "bore my sinful load" and "purchased for me peace with God."

You will never join Schwedler in his assessment of the cross if you never come to see your "sinful load." Sin is the greatest load in the world. What is sin? It is refusing to live the way God, our Creator and Ruler, wants us to live. It is thumbing our noses in His face and saying: "We don't care about how You want us to live. We will live the way we want to live."

God tells us that we must be one hundred per cent righteous before He will allow us to enter into heaven. Can you imagine meeting this God who demands that we be perfectly righteous? Can you imagine standing before him loaded down with your sin and guilt?

The fact is that our sins must be forgiven before we can ever enter the presence of God for eternity, and God cannot forgive our sins until the penalty He has pronounced on our sins is carried out. For God to forgive our sins without honoring that penalty would amount to His denying His own justice and compromising His character.

That brings us to the cross. It was there that Jesus took the penalty for sinners. He actually bore the "sinful load" there. The wrath of God against our sins was poured out on Him so that all who repent of their sins and believe in Him will never have to bear that penalty themselves.

Sin puts us at odds with God. But when sin is forgiven through Christ's atoning death, we have peace with God.

If you look at Jesus' death on the cross as just another man dying another death, Schwedler's hymn will sound absurd. But if you understand your "sinful load" and what Jesus did about it, you will gladly join him in singing:

What is faith's foundation strong?
What awakes my heart to song?
He who bore my sinful load,
Purchased for me peace with God,
Jesus Christ, the crucified.
This is the great thing I know:
This delights and stirs me so:
Faith in him who died to save,
Him who triumphed o'er the grave:
Jesus Christ, the crucified.

God's Glad Man

From God's Word, the Bible...

I waited patiently for the Lord;
And He inclined to me,
And heard my cry.
He also brought me up out of a horrible pit,
Out of the miry clay,
And set my feet upon a rock,
And established my steps.
He has put a new song in my mouth—
Praise to our God;
Many will see it and fear,
And will trust in the Lord.

Psalm 40:1-3

His name was Billy Bray. He was born in 1794 in a tin-mining community in southwestern England.

In his younger years, Billy lived, as he put it, "very near hell." He was such a drunkard that each night his wife would go to the tavern to help him home. He was such a blasphemer that his friends said his words came from hell itself because they smelled of sulfur.

But Billy Bray was converted to Christ in November of 1823, and praise to God became the dominant feature of his life. He would often say: "If they were to put me in a barrel, I would shout glory out through the plug-hole!"

Some of his friends scoffed at his conversion and suggested that he had gone mad. Here's how Billy responded: "They said I was a mad-man, but they meant I was a glad-man, and, glory be to God! I have been glad ever since."

Nearing his seventy-fourth birthday and feeling very ill, Billy went to a doctor. "You are going to die," the doctor somberly said. Upon receiving such news, many would sit in stunned silence. Others would break down and sob. Not Billy! He shouted: "Glory! Glory be to God! I shall soon be in heaven!"

Then Billy turned to the doctor and asked: "When I get up there, shall I tell them that you will be coming too?"

As wonderful and compelling as the story of Billy Bray is, it contains elements of danger. We must not be led astray by Billy Bray! One danger is to think that we must be as bad as he was before we need to be saved. This is the conclusion many draw. They think Christianity is only for those who have plumbed the depths of wickedness. The truth is we are all sinners, and, as such, we all need to be saved (Rom. 3:10,23). To put it another way, we all come into this world in a state of spiritual deadness. We are alive to sin but dead to God. Among dead people, there are degrees of decay, but there are no degrees of deadness. Dead is dead! The person who died a hundred years ago is more decayed than the one who died five minutes ago, but they are both dead. Some sinners are more decayed than others, but all are equally dead, and need, therefore, spiritual life from God.

The message of Christianity is clear—no one is too bad to be saved, and no one is too good to be saved!

Another danger is to think that we must be exactly like Billy Bray after we are saved. Conversion to Christ doesn't obliterate our personalities. Those who are quiet and reserved before they are saved will manifest those qualities after they are saved. And those who, like Billy, are exuberant by nature will show that same exuberance after they are saved.

But while Christians have differing personalities, they have this in common—the element of praise. While each will express that praise in keeping with his or her personality type, it will be present. Every Christian can say of the Lord:

He has made me glad, He has made me glad,
I will rejoice for he has made me glad.
He has made me glad, He has made me glad,
I will rejoice for he has made me glad.

The other side of the coin is this: we shouldn't be too quick to use our personality types to excuse ourselves from more exuberant praise. It could be that Billy's life of praise was not so much a product of his personality as it was of his understanding. In other words, he might very well have praised God more exuberantly for salvation than others because he understood salvation more than they. The explanation for Billy Bray may be that he let the words of Isaiah 12:1-2 sink more deeply into his mind and heart than most of us ever will:

O Lord, I will praise You;
Though You were angry with me,
Your anger is turned away, and You comfort me.
Behold, God is my salvation,
I will trust and not be afraid;
"For YAH, the Lord, is my strength and my song;
He also has become my salvation."

The Shot That Was Never Fired

From God's Word, the Bible...

The lot is cast into the lap,
But its every decision is from the Lord.

The king's heart is in the hand of the Lord,
Like the rivers of water;
He turns it wherever He wishes.

The horse is prepared for the day of battle,
But deliverance is of the Lord.

Proverbs 16:33; Proverbs 21:1; Proverbs 21:31

A Union soldier had guard duty one night. He watched and watched, but he didn't see. What was it that he didn't see? A Confederate soldier pointing his rifle at him! The trigger was never pulled. The shot was never fired. The Union soldier was spared. And the name of the spared soldier? It was none other than Ira D. Sankey. Sankey, the famous gospel singer? Yes, one and the same.

What was it that caused the Confederate soldier not to fire the deadly shot? Amazingly enough, Sankey began singing a hymn just as the soldier was about to squeeze the trigger, and the hymn was none other than the Confederate's favorite. So he listened a while, stole away in the night, and Sankey lived.

It's not enough to merely say Sankey lived. How he lived! He went on to be associated with D. L. Moody. He sang in Moody's crusades, and in so doing brought blessing to multitudes of people.

Sankey never knew how close he came to death that night until years later. It was Christmas Eve of 1876, and Sankey was on board a boat on the Delaware River. Someone recognized him, and immediately several crowded around to ask if he would sing a Christmas hymn. For some reason Sankey chose not to sing a Christmas song but rather *Savior, Like a Shepherd Lead Us.*

When Sankey finished singing, a man approached to ask a series of questions. Had he, Sankey, served in the Union army? Yes. Did he remember having guard duty at a particular place in 1862? Yes. Did he remember singing that very song while on guard duty? Yes. It was then that Sankey learned about the shot that was not fired.

It would certainly have been a great loss if Sankey had been killed on the night that he was posted to watch. So what about that shot that was never fired? How are we to explain it? Was it only a remarkable coincidence that Sankey began to sing at the precise moment that his life was hanging in the balance? Was it another remarkable coincidence that he chose to sing the Confederate soldier's favorite hymn? Many would say so. But Christians do not believe in coincidence. They believe in providence.

Providence is God managing and controlling even the smallest circumstances to the glory of His name and the good of His people.

The sparing of Sankey's life was certainly a kind providence. It's obvious to us that God had important work for Sankey to do. But there are also those providences which Christians call "strange" or "hard." These are providences that don't make sense to us. They are those in which God sends difficulties into the lives of His people. Great faith dares to believe that even God's hard providences are kind, that even in them God has our best interests at heart and is working for our good.

At the time, it may have seemed a hard providence for Paul to have his path blocked while he was seeking to advance God's kingdom. Having to be in Troas was not what he wanted. There were many other difficult circumstances he faced—shipwrecks, beatings, persecutions to name just a few! His words in Acts 14:22 still apply today: "We must through many tribulations enter the kingdom of God." In it all, he knew from the words God gave him, Romans 8:28, that ". . .all things work together for good to those who love God, to those who are the called according to His purpose."

The hard providences of life should cause us to love the words of Charles A. Tindley:

Trials dark on every hand, And we cannot understand
All the ways that God would lead us
To that blessed promised land;
But He'll guide us with His eye, And we'll follow till we die;
We will understand it better by and by.

One of the most exquisite delights of heaven will be learning about the hard providences that came our way, and another will be learning about the same in the lives of others.

The supreme example of a hard providence is the one that God Himself endured. It was a hard providence that caused men to despise Jesus and nail Him to a cruel cross. But through that hard providence, God has provided salvation for all sinners who will turn away from sin and trust in Christ. Until we learn in heaven all the meanings of all God's providences, let us sing:

Savior, like a shepherd lead us,
Much we need Thy tender care. . .

Books Included in this Series

My Coffee-Cup Meditations includes the original individual volumes

A Dog and A Clock (Series#1)

The "Thumbs-Up" Man (Series#2)

When God Blocks Our Path (Series#3)

Fading Lines, Unfading Hope Series#4)

The Day the Milk Spilled (Series#5)

"Where Are the Donuts?" (Series#6)

Sure Signs of Heavenly Hope (Series#7)

My Dog Knows It's Sunday (Series#8)

Rover and the Cows (Series#9)

Apples of Gold in Silver Settings (Series#10)

Old Houses, New Houses (Series#11)

Golden Key and Silver Chain (Series#12)